AUTISM:

A NEW PERSPECTIVE

INSIDE THE HEART AND MIND OF A NON-VERBAL YOUNG MAN

By Andrea Libutti, MD and João Carlos

Cover photo by Sara Correia

Dedication:

This book is for all of the moms who work so diligently to improve the lives of their children. And especially to Helena, João's mother, who awakened to her own heart and by doing so, opened the door for her Soul doctor to shine. I am forever grateful to you.

Table of Contents

Foreword vii

About this book xiii

Section I: Letters From João..1

Introduction 2

Chapter 1: Autism Answers...4

What is it like to be autistic?.......................................4

How do we help the autism population?................................7

Why is autism so prevalent? 11

Is autism recovery possible? 12

Chapter 2: Autism Lessons 15

Is autism here to teach us something?................................15

What are the best schools for autism?................................17

Are autistic people telepathic?.....................................20

How can people recover from chronic illness?....................21

What happens when parents don't give
their children space? 23

Can we find peace on this planet?....................................24

Chapter 3: João's Autism...26

Do you feel disconnected from life?.................................26

How do you connect to higher beings?................................27

How did you learn English?..32

What would your ideal life be like as
an independent person?..33

Section II: João's Insights **37**

Chapter 4: The Nature of Autism and Life **38**

Chapter 5: Raising an Individual Afflicted
by Autism **45**

Chapter 6: Aloofness and Extreme Sensitivity **48**

Chapter 7: Behaviors: Tip-toeing, Screaming
and Repetition **54**

Chapter 8: Energetic Issues and Seizures **59**

Chapter 9: Communication **63**

Chapter 10: Children of Today **67**

Section III: João Answers Parents' Questions **81**

Introduction **82**

Chapter 11: Communication **84**

How can I help my 25-year old son
communicate more effectively? 84

How can I get my 11-year old son more
motivated to communicate with RPM
(Rapid Prompting Method)? 86

How do we get past objections to communicate, in my
minimally verbal son, because it's "too hard"? 89

How can we communicate with our 5-year
old grandson who is non-verbal with autism? 90

Chapter 12: Behaviors **93**

Why does my 12-year old son move around constantly -
jumping, twisting, vocalizing and more? 93

Why is my 12-year old son having such
difficulties sleeping? 95

Why does my highly sensitive 13-year old daughter have
bursts of energy in the evenings? 96

Chapter 13: Independence...**98**

How can I find meaningful direction for my
14-year old son with autism?..98

What can I do to support my twins with autism, to
make life on Earth easy, fulfilling and pleasant? 99

What either physical or spiritual, is my son's biggest
block to being neurotypical?...100

Why did my son become autistic and how
can I recover him?...101

Will my 13-year old non-verbal son have
an independent future?..103

Will my 15-year old son ever live
independently? 104

What are the most important aspects to include when
creating an organization to serve autistic individuals
with independence?...108

Chapter 14: Education **111**

Is a mainstream classroom the best option
for my 5-year old daughter?..111

Is my 17-year old severely autistic son
ready to learn to read and write?..112

What is the best option for a school for
my 6-year old son with autism?..115

Chapter 15: Aggression...**117**

Why does my 10-year old son become
aggressive and refuse to communicate,
and enjoy being treated like a baby?..................................117

How can I help my 14-year old son with
severe aggression towards our family? 118

Why has my 14-year old son suddenly
regressed and become very angry? 121

Chapter 16: Technology **123**

Why does my 12-year old son only
watch shows for 4-year olds and should
we limit his time on his iPad? 123

Should we restrict use of electronic devices
and light up toys for our son with autism? 125

My 13-year old son is obsessed with video games.
Is this because he is traumatized by the divorce
and he is avoiding his feelings? 126

Chapter 17: Mental Health **128**

Is my 9-year old son happy about the
biomedical interventions, therapy and
programs we are doing? 128

How can we reduce my 11-year old
daughter's anxiety? 129

What did I do wrong to cause my 9-year
old son to severely regress this past year? 132

How does a mother let go of grief
and sorrow? 134

Chapter 18: Wellness **136**

Why is my 9-year old son so resistant to
my suggestions for healthy food choices? 136

What is triggering the seizures in my
13-year old son? 138

What does my 10-year old daughter want
me to know about her wellbeing
and integration? 139

Why am I here? 141

How can I reconnect to my intuitive self? 143

Afterword **145**

FOREWORD

There is a powerful revolution happening within the field of autism that is transforming not only the way we see individuals with this diagnosis but hopefully the way we see ourselves. Until recently, many on the spectrum did not have the voice nor the support to share their awareness with the world. Many of them were locked in bodies that did not obey their commands and therefore were perceived as limited by those around them.

This began to change when facilitated communication gave those that are non-verbal the ability to share their wisdom and perceptions of reality with the world.

As a former Pediatric Speech Language Pathologist turned multidimensional communicator, I can assure you that what is being shared by João Carlos in this book is an opportunity for your own growth in awareness. In my experience, most professionals working with those on the spectrum, and their parents, genuinely want these individuals to be able to convey their wants, needs, and awareness, but are unprepared for or ill-equipped to deal with the reality shock of discovering that the awareness expressed is far beyond what they could have imagined. For example, what happens when the non-verbal individual begins to express that the education system does not suit them? Or that the medication prescribed for them is causing more harm than good? How do they respond when this once non-communicative individual starts expressing his or her awareness about higher orders of consciousness, skills such as telepathy, or deep empathy that do not jive with who they have perceived this person to be? Are they— are we?—still willing to listen?

What João Carlos shares in *Autism: A New Perspective* is not only true for him but also expresses a more profound truth: that what we *think* someone knows and what they actually have access to are two very different things. As you read his words, consider that this young man is revealing what it is like to *be* him. He is telling you what is supportive, and what is not. He is sharing how he functions and why. He's telling you these things not just so that you can better support him, and others like him, but so that you also can grow beyond any limiting perceptions of who he is.

The information in this book is an exciting invitation to the world of autism. It's an invitation worth accepting. How do I know this? Because two decades ago, children diagnosed with autism began to share their wisdom with me through telepathy, a means of communication which scientists are now proving to be common among those on the spectrum, and which João Carlos addresses so beautifully in this book.

These children shared their advanced perception of reality with me and their intentions to support us in seeing beyond our limited points of view about them. They fed me information about autism, which up to that point had not been explored, and helped me write my book *Awesomism: A New Way to Understand the Diagnosis of Autism*, which was published in 2008.

Back then, there were many books about autism written by professionals speaking through their lens regarding the needs of this population. At the time, the children shared with me that the challenge with the professional point of view was that no-one was able or willing to take the time to ask those on the spectrum if their theories where supportive. Thus the "experts" were shaping the field of autism as best they could, but again, based only on their lens.

Back when my book was published, it was a stretch to believe in the telepathic information shared by those diagnosed with autism. What I found, however, was that life became easier for them and their families when I applied the information they provided.

This information was to act as a bridge. In *Autism: A New Perspective*, we have the blessing of learning directly from someone living with the multifaceted skills and challenges of autism. You'll find that João Carlos offers his information not just from his mind and personal experience, but more importantly from his soul! As he shares his awareness—from the soul— he will open you to yours... if you allow it! For just as his co-creator of this book, Dr. Andrea Libutti is a medical doctor, João Carlos has a different kind of expertise—he is a doctor of your soul.

Before you jump in and start reading the wisdom shared in these pages, I have to speak to Dr. Andrea Libutti's role in getting João Carlos' message out into the world! As someone who has been speaking about the abilities and the awareness of those on the spectrum long before it was popular to do so, I have great appreciation and admiration for the clarity Dr. Libutti brings to the co-creation of both this book and the work of João Carlos. Dr. Libutti is not new to this conversation either. She is the mother of a child diagnosed with autism and thus has lived conversations in all its many facets. She's devoted her life to her child's well-being, and her professional career to finding answers that actually make a difference for all. She is unique as a medical professional, but not as a mother. Mothers will seek answers where others do not dare to tread. It does not surprise me that she found answers in her connections with João Carlos.

But what I love most about Dr. Andrea Libutti is that she is not afraid to place her medical credentials and wisdom side by side with the wisdom shared by her co-author, João Carlos. This is a powerful combination and I know you will evolve in body, mind, and soul because of the courage, love, and wisdom they both offer through *Autism: A New Perspective.*

Suzy Miller M.Ed.
Founder of the Awesomism Practitioner Process
Author of Awesomism: A New Way to Understand the Diagnosis of Autism
www.suzymiller.com

About this book

I would like to begin with the first auspicious letter that João wrote to me in 2016. His mother Helena and I, were already friends through email. She had read my book *Awakened by Autism* (Hay House, 2015), and reached out to me to collaborate as mothers of autistic children.

Here is what she wrote to me, about six months into our friendship:

> My Dear Friend,
>
> How are you? The reason I am writing to you today, is not to tell you about the last months' events, but rather to share with you a letter which João decided to write to you today.
>
> It is true that you have been on my mind quite often, and perhaps João picked up on that, for he reached out to me today asking to write. What follows are his words to you.

I have typed out his letter, but I am sending you the photos of his handwritten pages. João writes fluent English, so language is no problem if you wish to ask him anything.

Love,
Helena

Dear Dr. Andrea,

I am writing to let you know that you have been on my mind for quite some time. I am autistic and still facing great challenges, but my heart tells me that I shall overcome them…

I have been receiving messages that we need to join hands, and you and your son have already started your journey to healing.

On this side of the planet, a lot is yet to be done, but we can exchange ideas and experiences.

Dr. Andrea, as you write autism is a wake-up call to humanity, and it is up to us to bring about the change. I am looking forward to hearing from you.

Hugs from Portugal,
João Carlos

As you can imagine, I was shocked and amazed.

What has since transpired, is our collaboration to shift the old paradigm of autism, fraught with tragedy and despair, out of our mindset, so that a new perspective, a life-affirming message of hope and healing, can replace it.

I cannot begin to explain how this amazing young man holds the knowledge that he holds. It defies our common sense, and certainly cannot be backed by science, not in 2019 anyway.

I risk a lot of backlash for supporting this writing. But there is something inside of me that is demanding the completion of this project. Much like João's inner voice, my intuition knows that the information *must* be made available for those people who are ready for it, for this new perspective on autism.

I invite you to consider his messages, for no matter the ethereal source, what he espouses is a return to Love. We have become so disconnected from our inner selves, our true essence, that the only way back is to begin a journey of Self-Love, one individual at a time.

We cannot continue as a species, to destroy ourselves and our planet through fearful thinking and actions, and hope for a better tomorrow. The time is now, to begin the shift, first within ourselves, and what will follow will be a more peaceful and loving humanity.

And João assures us that when we do, our beloved children with autism will come around, will join us fully on this planet, as the sons and daughters that we so desperately want, but not until we create an environment that reflects the Love and compassion that they are here to anchor.

We long for the day when we know that our children's future is secure. That they will be happy, in meaningful relationships and careers, fully independent and able to live in this world without our support.

But here's the thing. These children want *us* to change, just as much as we want them to change. And the exquisite paradox of this autism journey, is that when we let go of our need to force them to be more like us, we create space for them to become the truly magnificent individuals they are here to become – which is far better than anything we can imagine.

I have structured the book into three sections. The first section is a series of questions that I asked João, specifically about his experience living with autism, and his broader thoughts about the autism epidemic and how to help our children.

The second section covers the topics that he chose to write about, to help parents better understand behaviors, and what parents must do to help their children.

The third section is a compilation of questions that parents asked João about their own challenges with their children, and his responses.

I hope you will find peace in the pages of this book, and great hope, not only for our children but for ourselves.

Every time I read and reread what João has to say, I am overcome with emotion at the simplicity and Love behind his words.

May your journey be filled with ease, and when it is not, may you find the courage to keep going, never giving up on yourself, just as you would never give up on your child.

Andrea Libutti

SECTION I

· · · · · · · · · · ● ● ● ● ● ● ● ● ● ● · · · · · · · · ·

LETTERS FROM JOÃO

Introduction

When João and I agreed to write a book together, I had no idea that the very important information we would share with the world, would be so profoundly healing for me. As I compiled all of the information he shared over the past several years, I often found myself in tears, feeling enormous gratitude and proximity to the Divine.

While João will tell you we all hold the Divine within ourselves, it is incredibly difficult in this day and age, to remember that and to connect with it. This book will help you remember.

What follows in this first section, are a series of questions that I posed to João, and his candid responses. I left his greetings and closings intact, because I thought it would be easier on the reader to maintain the pace and assimilate each concept. I also edited very little, because I wanted his voice to remain authentic.

We all have our own beliefs about the world. For some of you, what you will read in these pages, will feel like blasphemy. Please accept our apologizes in advance, for our intention is only to promote a return, of every human being, to the Love that they are, so we can all live in peace and harmony.

For all of you scientifically minded souls, all I can say is that Galileo was considered a heretic in his time, for his views. He spent the latter part of his life under house arrest. In history, how many scientists were outcast for their "unscrupulous" ideas, that did not match the thinking of their time?

And Joan of Arc, the 18-year old commander in chief of the French army, who talked to Angels and undoubtedly had Divine guidance, was burned at the stake. We are afraid of new ideas, sometimes violently so.

Please don't burn me at the stake.

CHAPTER 1

Autism Answers

What is it like to be autistic?

Dear Dr. Andrea,

As you know, autism affects both the mind and the body. As far as the body is concerned, autism is very debilitating and painful. My body does not feel as numb as it used to, but it is still very toxic and there are many urges within me to clean it up.

Quantifying the toxic burden is not entirely possible, but there demands a lot of detoxing. That and getting me out of this prison, which is spending my days at home most of the time with nothing worthwhile to do. It is as if my body is imprisoned twice.

When autistic individuals are aware of the extent of their limitations, life can sometimes be too demanding and we yearn for death. When I was seventeen, I went through a very difficult phase in my life. In fact, life has been a real challenge and it was not always something that I wanted to face.

As time went by, I did not see my body recover as I wished it would, and I had to live everyday with maladaptation, together with a mind that was unable to express itself because of a numbed body. When I was that age and did not see things improve, I developed anxiety.

As a soul in this life, I wanted to contribute towards the awakening of people on this planet, and to become a Soul doctor, but the changes meant to take place did not occur and I became desperate.

On this plane, my first epileptic episode occurred. I wanted to go Home and did not want my mother to deter me, for when people are too bonded to one another, their excessive chords of dependency can delay the will of the soul to break away from its body. Fortunately, my mother was aware of this and did not cause pressure in any way.

As it was not my time however, the Masters united in order to decide if after all, I should return Home. What they decided was to delay my departure, and so I am still striving with autism and the need to accomplish my life mission.

As an autistic individual and non-verbal, I have managed to observe and gain insights which otherwise, I might not have. At the same time despite my challenges, being able to communicate through writing, gets people to question the information and that is part of the awakening process of those around me. As time goes by, we can see that more and more people are questioning things and as we hold hands and stretch them out, we can move to the Light.

My body needs a holistic approach to healing and I am focusing on it as common practice. We should avoid eating non-organic food and increase our intake of fruits and vegetables. As you know, what we eat influences are healing and mood, and most of the time, our energy levels vary according to the food we eat.

When my diet is not wholesome, my body suffers with bloating and with teeth grinding. When we fail to acknowledge the importance of food on physical and mind wellbeing, we miss out on a lot. Our bodies need to be fed physically and mentally too.

Autism causes many counter-indications and information which is contradictory to our wholesome recovery, or restoring our wellbeing. It is not only important to clean our diet, but also to clean the mind-forms which are toxic.

These thoughts that we catch from those around us, who do not alter their perception towards autism and what it is here to show, tend to slow down the process of autism accomplishing its cry for a change to humanity.

We are highly sensitive and having to deal with a burdened body and burdened mind, through exposure to toxic thoughts and toxic people, increases our pain. This explains why schools are so demanding most of the time.

There is a great disbelief in the autistic population and what they can achieve on the whole. It is something which society has failed to address with interest and an open mind.

Love,
João

How do we help the autism population?

Dear Dr. Andrea,

I am delighted to share my thoughts with you so dementia gone undiagnosed can be healed. I am not talking about people with disabilities or mental disorders, but of people considered normal, but unwilling to change or move out of their ego. Let us bring some Light.

What do we have to do to help the autism population?

First of all, it has to be once and for all erased, the idea that autistic individuals are not present. To the outside, it may look like it, but it is not true.

Autistic individuals are in refusal to settle in a world, where there is much pain and disbelief in brotherhood. Mankind has moved away from the values of kindness and compassion, and autism is a cry to humanity to move back to the energy of Love and compassion.

Autistic individuals on a soul level, are vibrating in Love and they are still very much connected to it. What they see and fear on this Earth, is pain and lack of Love, so there is a refusal to ground. However, because they are highly sensitive and empathic, they breathe in the pain, and their body becomes burdened in this energy. The pain is excruciating for the individual.

As all of us should know, thought forms are highly toxic when negative, therefore autism invites humanity to look into this issue, especially when it comes to cleaning up our energy field. As we all are connected to extremely high stress levels of today's current cities, this leads people to become anxious and depressed. Autism shows those features too.

Life is an asset and demands that humanity value it, and move back to a sound lifestyle in respect and union with nature. Autism wants Earth and mother nature to be in harmony, and people have forgotten about that. Autism also requires authenticity, and if we feel that the truth is being withheld, our pain increases and we seek to withdraw.

Autistic individuals are much connected to Light source, and will not ground as citizens of this planet if major changes do not occur.

To sum up, the autism population hopes for a reversal of damage brought upon humanity through greed and the urge for power. Autism is a wake-up call to humankind, that values like authenticity in all areas can be regained. In Love we vibrate, in Love we wish to vibrate.

If you ask me what parents and teachers can do, I shall tell you that change always comes from within, and it starts one individual at a time. Start within the household by bringing the family closer. All mothers have a crucial role as child bearers, and if they begin the process of first liberating the pain they carry in their wombs, they can start liberating a little of us too.

As mother's clear away their pain, and that which they carry of ancestors, the first spark of hope is ignited. The changes within the household will inevitably occur because their inner Light is stronger, and because of this they will cater to their health and emotional wellbeing, because their vibration has increased. This simple process of energy clearing of the womb will bring about changes. As women, they will want to connect to their Divine, and that is only possible by cleaning up their diet and taking care of their emotions.

As we all know emotions can be a pathway to healing or to disaster. As we are connected, we vibrate also according to the places and people that surround us. When mothers are conscious of this fact, by looking after themselves they start the ripple effect of change.

First in all homes, and then moving forth to teachers and schools, for they are responsible for the education of their children. Teachers are also of crucial importance, and it is crucial that they come to accept the spiritual nature that is part of the human being.

Schools have to draw away from an industrial perspective of education, to embrace a more humanistic approach and cater first, to the physical, emotional and spiritual wellbeing of students. Looking at education with subjects in different drawers, is totally devoid of meaning and relevance when it comes to building knowledge.

Much Love,
João Carlos

Why is autism so prevalent?

Dear Dr. Andrea,

Thank you, courageous friend, for your words and wisdom ready to share with the world.

I have been receiving desires to share with you, what constantly comes to my mind. As you know autism is on the rise, but it does not *only* have to do with the heavy pollution of planet Earth. Of course, it does contribute towards the picture, but there is a whole lot more going on.

In the first place, dear friend, people who reincarnate on this planet and who suffer from autism, are old souls who volunteered to come to Earth and raise its vibration. But being on planet Earth is such a tough school, that many do not wish to be grounded or rather are reluctant to, if there is not a change in terms of vibration.

There have to be changes within the family unit, beginning with mothers, for real changes to occur. I have faced my ups and downs, and as a child I definitely did not want to be here. This planet is still very dense and backward, for people still need the spoken word to communicate.

There are other planets as you know, and we are not alone. We are multidimensional beings and exist on other

11

planes and dimensions. As you know many children with autism are non-verbal or considered so like me, but what is going on is essentially a mismatch of vibration.

We are connected to beings on other solar systems, and communication is through telepathy. When on planet Earth, we verify that this planet is still not evolved as it should be, and that most individuals are disconnected from their soul.

Besides having a sensitive body, which cannot take so much toxicity, we have to endure the pain of facing a world of ongoing individualism and lack of tolerance.

As more autistic individuals come to the forefront, societies have the opportunity to learn more. In each household, where Love and acceptance prevail, vibrations increase and a match with autistic individuals´ energy can be gained, and hands held, giving rise to a humanity that lives according to values of Love and trust.

Hugs from Portugal,
João Carlos

Is autism recovery possible?

Dear Dr. Andrea,

I want to share with you what happens to the human being who hasn't awakened. Autism is associated with the concept of aloofness, but this attitude reaches beyond the syndrome. Some truly believe that autism is the absence of the individual, but things are more complex than they may seem, and we cannot speak of such linearity in truth.

Aloofness has to do with an imbalance of the chakra system, especially the root chakra, but there are also spiritual reasons behind it. Humanity has deviated throughout time, from its true essence and soul, and has focused its look on materialism and what is external.

The growing number of children suffering from autism is symptomatic, and mirrors society and its lifestyle. The autistic individual announces that a new humanity has to find a balance between the Divine and the dense material world.

The autistic individual reaches for the Divine with great ease, because its soul does not wish to be on this plane. The Love that autistic individuals receive on Earth, helps their soul to accept reincarnation, and therefore recovery can be achieved with Love and perseverance.

Autism has to do with spiritual, energetic and physical issues. The same happens with Alzheimer's patients. The only difference is that autism begins early in life, and Alzheimer's at a much later stage.

Alzheimer's disease enables people to draw away from a reality, which they can see with little ease. The human being isn't just matter, but a soul which proposed to go through a certain amount of experiences, and as life develops, he/she sees how much he/she has come close to or deviated from that purpose.

The physical body reacts to suppressed emotions and shows them through disease. Alzheimer's patients feel that the dense planet did not allow them the connection to the omniscience of the soul, and the Light within fades. They retreat and take refuge in a body that does not desire vitality.

Like autism, Alzheimer's patients are able to live with their backs, half turned to the world.

Hugs from Portugal,
João Carlos

CHAPTER 2

Autism Lessons

Is autism here to teach us something?

Dear Dr. Andrea,

I have just read your message, and that is really the way to go. Changing beliefs and the mindset of the system on the whole, beginning within the household and caretakers, is the way to go. In fact, the idea of a need to fix, gives rise to a new question which is, who is here to fix who?

Is it the parents who are to fix their child with autism? Or is it the child with autism, who is appealing first to parents and to their caretakers and teachers, to go back to regaining their true power and potential, through a change of beliefs and lifestyle habits?

Have you noticed the wonder of gaze of children with autism? Many of them, who are not numbed by drugs, have a glow that shines through their look or gaze, and that is the purity of their inner light and connectedness to soul coming through.

Individuals with autism either refuse to be grounded, opting for a drawn back look, or we see individuals with their high sensitivity. There is no middle term when it comes to autism, and there is more to the picture.

On the whole, autism is rising. To say that this is due to the fact that the spectrum is wide, and the medical establishment is more aware, is just a nice way to sweep things under the carpet.

Nature does not err, and it is not like they say, that we have to save planet Earth, but rather we have to save ourselves, starting with the enlightenment of each individual. Individuals with autism are highly connected to their souls and all that is.

The invitation of autism is this: how connected do you as parents want to be, and then as a society too? The planet does not need to be saved, because nature is perfect. But if we do not alter our treatment towards it, we will be swallowed in its uproar during its search for equilibrium and balance.

The same can be said about autism. Numbers will continue to rise, and either individuals will reclaim their birthright and power within, raising their vibration, or humanity will succumb in its own refusal to live a life of grace and Love for all individuals and all that is.

You can count on me, for all in which you think I might be of help.

Love and gratitude,
João Carlos

What are the best schools for autism?

My dear friend Dr. Andrea,

I will now focus on my point of view regarding the school system. First of all, I can confidently share that education is killing motivation to learn, and the curiosity of the learner. My years at school were painful for many reasons. One of them was the fact that schools are mostly cold places both socially and in terms of facilities.

I remember the classrooms painted in white and grey with desks lined up in rows. The teacher would talk away, reciting content concerning the subjects, and the students had a hard time keeping attention, sitting still and taking notes.

I used to comfortably get away, by deviating with the mind, but at times the boredom was such that I just wanted to scream and leave, and sometimes, most often, I did.

I believe in schools without walls, in which each experience is a learning opportunity. If constant input is given in a natural manner, then learning becomes an easy and smooth process. Of course, opportunities then have to be given or created for the student to show what he has learned, and built on.

I would suggest that students be given projects, or that they come up with their own, showcasing the knowledge they have acquired.

(From another letter)

When it comes to school, then things really get tough. Schools function mostly as industries, piling students into crates after they have been conditioned, or then programmed to fit into the natural order of things, without questioning.

Most schools don't cater to the needs of their students, but rather to the system. They are places of pain for both students and teachers, who haven't been completely taken by the system. On the whole, schools are energetically dense places with seemingly automated students and teachers, teaching knowledge in between bell rings.

Andrea, does this make any sense to you? Can you tell me why most schools murder a student's will, or motivation to learn and construct knowledge? As human beings, we have the ability to think and construct knowledge, if we are guided to. But most schools continue to pour out knowledge, sometimes outdated, and insist on memorization.

When it comes to my personal experience, school was a daunting experience because I had a label of autism, was non-verbal and had poor motor skills. All these ingredients put together gave teachers the illusion, or opened the way to an excuse, that I did not have the ability to learn or even wanted to at all. Most of the time, I had to endure classes which were totally desire-less for any being with the slightest ability to think.

What I think should be done regarding schools, is that first of all, we should look after and cater to the wellbeing of human beings, each with their individuality and each of their needs have to be met. Teachers need to be there to guide us or show us the way when we are lost, but it is up to us to construct knowledge.

As students, we have to be exposed to knowledge in a variety of fields. In the end, we should present a project where we applied the knowledge we gained, and constructed knowledge giving back to society, the investment made.

I can tell you that schools, generally speaking in my point of view, do more harm than good to human beings, reinforcing the ego and weakening the heart.

Love,
João Carlos

Are autistic people telepathic?

Dear Dr. Andrea,

As you might be expecting, I am writing to you to tell you what is on my mind. As you may know, communication can be through speech, both oral and written, but also through telepathy.

As most people have forgotten it, this skill has to be re-learned, but individuals with autism can still communicate through this manner, although it may not be picked up on, because of how closed people have become towards their innate abilities. As we go along however, and more and more awaken, this means of communication will become more common.

As you know, another thing that I must do, is to get the word out to humanity to raise its vibration. We can no longer persist in doing things the way we have, and raising consciousness is essential.

My seizures have reduced, but there is a lot of energy within me, in need of being expelled, and because it isn't, my anxiety increases intensely and so do my levels of frustration. I love writing but because as you know, I need the support of my mother's hand, I cannot do it as often as demanded by the Angels.

Angels are energy and evolved consciousness, and they whisper in my ear. But as always, dependency leads to refrain from doing what we wish.

My dear friend, these are the words that my heart demands to share.

Blessings from the Angels,
João Carlos

How can people recover from chronic illness?

Dear Dr. Andrea,

I now want to talk with you about issues that affect the ill, and it has to do with the need to alter the energy patterns of surrounding people. The sick person displays physical, emotional and energetic issues. For recovery to take place, there is a need for a change of thoughts, beliefs and behavior within the family unit, otherwise the disease or illness continues to thrive on toxic energy.

I would like you to understand that the energy pattern that led to the imbalance has to be broken. The person who is ill is aware, and feels the energy of those around him or her. If the prevailing energy is of conflict, disbelief and of arguing, then it clings to the sick person's auric field.

All illness is an invitation for an individual to change, and to change the surrounding environment. The places where people live and work, also need to be cleared and worked on, for there is energetic information in them.

Everything is energy and has an energetic label. As you will understand, a sick person has a weak immune system and much fear. All these energy issues which I have mentioned, come into play and must be addressed for recovery.

The way illness has been addressed in these past few years, needs to be reevaluated and a new paradigm set. I consider it fundamental, that humankind awakens and becomes conscious that we are all connected, and recovery and cure is interdependent with this connection.

Love,
João Carlos

What happens when parents don't give their children space?

Dear Andrea,

How are you, my lovely friend? I can tell you that I am excited to be with you and that the holiday break was good for me and my mom, because we managed to rest and be apart peacefully.

Many times, parents of autistic children or other conditions, cling too much to their children and in their urge to protect, stifle them. Clinging onto someone continuously, is an energy based on fear that someone is indispensable, and that the other has no means of survival. Clinging onto someone stifles them, and creates energetic chords of dependence and fear, and the energy is blocked of both the child and the parent.

All souls are on Earth to have a human experience, and the energy of fear limits and stifles. I can also add, that the energy of fear that prevails in relationships between parents and children suffering various conditions, is not exclusive to this type of relationship, but prevails in other types such as husband and wife or other.

Love is the energy of freedom to choose and heed our path, and to feel the breeze as we go.

Having been away from my mother, gave both of us space, and we felt ensured that each of us can survive apart, and meet and engage with other souls waiting to grow and exchange experiences and Love.

Andrea, as you see I am open to follow my path and my mother is ready to let me go with the energy of Love in her heart.

I am ready for our work together.

Love Andrea to you,
João Carlos

Can we find peace on this planet?

My dear Andrea,

I wish you first of all, much Love. Can we find peace in our lives on this planet? The answer is yes, and we shall achieve it even though there are moments of great distress and pain.

The planet we live on is very dense and demanding, and our egos are often in the way, impeding us of seeing the full picture. On our planet Earth, the ego is much in the way of us getting to feel peace and tranquility whatever the circumstances.

What I can tell you is that all is well, and after living this moment, you are to start a new cycle in your life and

Heaven is with you. There is a new Andrea to emerge which is incompatible with the life and energy, until now. Trust the process my beautiful friend, and trust that you are being protected and guided.

As to us being together and giving consultations as a Soul doctor on my part, and counselling and coaching on your part with my mother, it is time to move ahead.

My charming soul sister I Love you,
João Carlos

CHAPTER 3

João's Autism

Do you feel disconnected from life?

Dear Dr. Andrea,

The first question that you ask about feeling disconnected, is easy to explain because there are many careless undertakings, when it comes to autism.

A lot of what is said and done regarding autism, is done on the basis of outsiders' viewpoints, or assumptions of what autism is, and not what individuals with autism feel or need.

We as individuals, are colors of a rainbow with different needs. What is often done, is that we are pressed into a baking tin, that is always the same shape and dough. The baker sees the customers are not all satisfied, some talk about their allergies, but he continues baking the same way, in the hope that his customers get used to his baking.

That explains what most of my life has been like, trying to fit all of me into a preconceived idea of what may be the best for me, even if the response is always showing the opposite.

As long as I can recall, people in general do not look at me, but at my autism. Even though they see that autism varies from individual to individual, they stick to assumptions of what they have heard.

This has led to bridges not being crossed, or arms held, and in the end, it is the weaker part who loses, because he is part of the minority, and the label lets the other off easily.

As you can see Dr. Andrea, it is easy to understand how it comes down to feeling discarded.

Love,
João Carlos

How do you connect to higher beings?

Dear Dr. Andrea,

We can connect with higher beings. As for me it is not a very complex process, for if demanded, desire takes over me and mentally I call upon the Masters, Archangels or Angels.

All these are energy consciousness, vibrating at higher levels than us as human beings. We all have the power and ability to connect and communicate with higher beings, but we have to allow ourselves.

Most people that I observe don't have faith, or do not believe in higher beings, and therefore allowance does not present itself. As children, we move around dimensions and tune in and out with ease, but then with programming, we shut down.

Autistic individuals are often left unaltered because of their features, that they pick up whatever is around them. When it comes to me then, you can understand how I have this characteristic as an individual with non-verbal autism and poor motor skills.

I have been neglected and put aside, and my ability to observe that around me has been great, and the ability to connect left almost intact.

When I am alone or willing, I just tune into the realm of the higher beings, and then mentally listen to what they tell me. Sometimes they present themselves visually and then I see colors.

Andrea, we are all connected and what I am told, can be picked up by someone who wants to and then sets the intention to do so.

Our cerebrum holds the power to communicate with other realms, and the more we tune in to it, the easier it gets. My messages come across easily, though most of the time I do not set the intention.

It comes naturally to me in thought form, and demands that I get it out of my system. When that doesn't happen, then a lot of energy accumulates in my system. When a lot of information does not manage to find an outlet, I increase the rate of my seizures.

My seizures demand further development. When I had my first seizure, I was seventeen. I was very emotionally stressed and soul hurt, because demands for the recovery of my physical body weren't being met, and that made me want to leave this planet.

After the first seizure, I was very fragile both physically and emotionally, and then came a phase of nightmares. As you know, there are Light beings and others from the shadow, and I began to suffer energy attacks, to further deploy me of any remaining abilities, or to minimize urges to accomplish my life mission.

The times that followed were tense and dark. My mother always protected me to the extent of her knowledge, but she was alone and unable to face the raging ocean.

I was alone wanting to die and unable to give my mother peace. As time went by, my seizures transformed from energy attacks from shadow beings, to energy activations.

When the Masters decided that I remain on Earth, and to support my life mission, my body had to be prepared for my healing work.

As you know my mission is to become a Soul doctor and practice holistic medicine, and my recovery shall show the world that there are no limits to the power of God within. I am still very much dependent, but the years to come are to be a complete turnover.

Andrea, you are part of my soul family, and circumstances which might seem completely arbitrary have brought us together.

Love,
João Carlos

Dear Andrea,

Can we carry on with our work? I can, as foreseen, continue to carry on the messages concerning autism and healing, for that is part of my purpose.

Although there seems to be a vacuum in my life now, I am being worked on energetically by evolved consciousness which some may call Angels. These beings which vibrate at a much faster rate and in other planes or dimensions, are ready to assist us. All we have to do is call upon them.

There are many ways to call upon help from Light beings from other realms. Whatever you feel is the right way for you, is the first way to connect. Whether you make use of a prayer you know or your own words, what prevails is your clear intention and the ability to connect the heart to the mind.

Calling upon evolved beings or consciousness can be made by addressing the Angels or Archangels by their names, or simply saying what we need and asking for the Angels that specialize in that field.

For instance, "Angels of wellbeing, please help me make choices that help me increase my physical wellbeing, by clearing the energy blocks that hinder my progress." All is then taken care of, if you are willing to connect and accept.

One of the things that keeps people from accepting what they ask for, is their unwillingness to accept, for they do not let go and they keep their ego and rational mind in the way. One must ask and trust, and that means letting go.

If you keep hooked on to what you think ought to be the outcome, tension is created and you impede the outcome, or slow it down, or to be more precise, become too distracted to acknowledge the signs and make the right choices.

One of the things that I want to add is that you can invoke help from other planets and galaxies too. The method is the same. All you have to do is ask for help with clear and heartfelt intention.

"Beings or Consciousness of Light and Love, I ask you to come to me and in the presence of Divine Love assist me in overcoming this challenge."

Can we go on with our endeavors, my dear Andrea and soul sister?

Love,
João Carlos

How did you learn English?

Dear Dr. Andrea,

At the moment, my days are spent killing time for I cannot go anywhere. As can be understood from my other letter, there is nowhere for me to go, where at least something interesting can be done. My mother is struggling and my father doesn't care much about my wellbeing, so it's up to my mother to keep on going.

I spend my days at home watching TV, either with my grandmother or with my father, when my mother goes to work. When she is at home and she has time, then I can write or go out. I like to be with my mother, but we have to learn to be apart. When we can be alone, then I can set off to accomplish my mission, which is far beyond this small country.

When it comes to telling you how I learned English, there isn't much to say. I simply tune into my English "I". As you know there are multiple realities, and we all have the ability to tune into our different "I" version. As demanded from my personal need and urge, I have practiced tuning into my English version of self, to be able to communicate internationally, but this ability has to be further perfected for other instances.

Love,
João Carlos

What would your ideal life be like as an independent person?

Dear Dr. Andrea,

Can you please help me and other autistic individuals, to also have a place in society? My life is so boring with nothing to do, day in and day out. We have to come up with something, because we cannot keep on at home with nothing worthwhile to do.

I personally would like to have something to do, and I am sure others would too. Can you consider setting up a special place where autistic individuals can thrive both physically and spiritually?

You have asked me before how I envision my days, and therefore I am going to share my thoughts. I would like to go to a place with nature around it. Every day, after waking up and having taken breakfast, I would go out for a walk in the forest or by the sea.

As you know, the sea is very soothing and salt water is full of minerals and other nutrients. Another reason for my reference to the sea, is that we are essentially water, and hydration plays a key role in the healing process. If we invoke the Goddess of the seas, the sea will be even more beneficial because then we can connect and become one, and vitality and health increase substantially.

In my case the connection is powerful because I have already lived in Atlantis. Many people do not believe in the existence of Atlantis, but it is a connection that I hold from past lives, and that is still encoded in my cells and memories. When I am at the sea, I feel at home and enlightened.

Getting back to what my day would be like, after the sea or stroll in nature, I would come back and do art work with my friends. I would paint with them, not necessarily the art most would expect, but art that flows from the soul without drawbacks. Then I would write about it and get the soul to express itself in another manner. The soul has many ways of coming through. We just have to allow it. My writing is a means of expression of my soul.

There has been very little investment in me, for not only do I have a label, but my body is also very toxic, and I have trouble concentrating and keeping still. At times, I lose control and that makes people give up on me easily.

After my writing, going back to my day, I would have lunch, which would be part of my clean diet. In the afternoon, I would listen to videos on all sorts of subjects, and then think about what my conclusions are, and how I could apply them in real life, showcasing them as my project.

Love,
João Carlos

SECTION II

. . . .

JOÃO'S INSIGHTS

CHAPTER 4

The Nature of Autism and Life

It is important that we look at autism from a new viewpoint and perspective. A lot has been written and said about the topic, but much of it is from the standpoint of the outsider.

It is high time that changes are brought about, and that will only occur if more individuals speak out to the crowd. Of course, communication is a handicap or deficit regarding autism, but having difficulties of expression does not mean we do not understand, or do not have a say.

Autism locks a mind in a body.

We may understand, hear or feel, and instruct our brain to respond, but our limbs fail and the tongue remains dead and stiff. We eagerly want to share an opinion, or respond to a question, but both our body and people around us, deafen or play deaf.

One of the most urgent things to be done, is to create opportunities from the outside for individuals afflicted by autism. How can this be done?

After all these years in which autism has locked us in our own skin, and making us dreaded outcasts, some advances have been made. Some individuals on the spectrum have been able to voice their concerns autonomously, and others with some kind of support, are managing to have a say. It is specifically about the latter that I wish to speak.

Looking back on my own past, despite all the challenges I still have to face, if my mother had given up on me, I would most likely be a mere accidental survivor on this planet, looked upon either as a curse, a punishment for former wrongdoings, or someone who is pitied on.

In our society, individuals like me and others that do not conform to normality, are still not very much accepted, but all have a right and mission to be here on this planet, and not one is grander than the other, or more important.

ON THE SOULS MISSION

As souls, we reincarnated with a mission, and experiences that we are willing to undergo in order to accomplish it. When souls are ready to reincarnate, they make agreements with other souls that are either going to hinder their process, or give us a hand.

Whatever sides souls take on Earth as people, all are working on the energy of Love, whether it is of a purer nature or not. All are working together, in order to help us fulfill our mission.

On Earth, we feel rage and pain when we feel hurt. Instead of reacting, what we should do is draw on our consciousness and awareness. It is true that in the middle of the storm, we give in and feel the rage of the vicious winds, but after some practice and after awakening, our views and perspective regarding the unfolding of events change.

Once again, going back to my own experiences, and with a different energy as to the difficult phases, especially concerning the school years, I can see the blessing behind those who did not put an effort to my betterment as a student, or inclusion in the system.

Of course, those moments were painful, and it hurt having teachers looking at me as a burden and not worth a penny of investment. But that just showed me that the way is not to swim endlessly against the current and lose energy and life, but rather turn the vicious beast into a source of inspiration.

ON FEAR

When we reincarnate, we are all going to have multiple experiences that are really going to push us, and in some instances really push us hard. But it is important not to dwell too long on the energy of fear, such as rage and hate.

Instead stop, and if you need to get rid of that energy because it is stifling, go to a place where you can scream and shout, and then transform the energy of the situation that left you imbalanced.

It is important that you do not block emotions, because by doing so you are blocking the flow of energy in your body. Sooner or later suppressed emotions and feelings, open space or ground for blocked energy, and crystallized energy becomes cysts and nodules, and disease settles in. Many ailments and diseases have to do with suppressed feelings and emotions.

We have to keep in mind, that on planet Earth we find the energies of duality. Being on this planet means having a human expression and therefore experiences, where different people, contexts and situations, give rise to different feelings and emotions.

When it comes to the feelings of bliss no one complains, but when we are experiencing the other side of the coin things change radically. What is important, is not to dwell too long on the energy of fear.

As humans, we are not always in control of the way we feel, but if we are conscious that we are spiritual beings having a human experience, we will feel it is okay at times to feel down, hurt or in pain.

It is also important that we live in that energy consciously, but then walk out of it. To dwell continuously on the energy of fear, contributes towards the growth of that energy, leading to depression, and it puts you in the place of victim.

ON DISEASE

When you are too long in this energy, entering a place of non-ability to walk out on your own, your immune system suffers and the body responds with different imbalances, which are called diseases.

The place where emotions are blocked or suppressed, develop symptoms of malfunction, which is the way of the body drawing your attention, that you are holding onto a negative emotion and are not allowing the flow of energy.

When we fall ill, or our body gives us signs of being unwell, we go to the doctor and await the diagnosis. We wait for someone exterior to ourselves, to tell us why a part of our body isn't responding appropriately.

The doctor will write out a prescription with medication, which you expect will help you and it may seem to for a while. But unless you change your energy and energy patterns, the solution is temporary. Medication might help you at least in the immediate timeline, but it will not be a solution in the long run.

Your body will continue to give signs of imbalance, and the former imbalance will prevail, and another part of your body will have become vulnerable. Things will continue this way until you decide to do your part.

No one is able to heal anyone, if there isn't permission on the part of that person, and the willingness to take responsibility for its importance throughout the process. What needs to be done is to take full responsibility.

There is one thing that we should keep in mind, and that is, that we have to take full responsibility for our well-being, or lack of it. Whatever we attracted, is because of our frequency or vibration. If we keep this in mind we will know that the same way we attracted something less pleasant in our life, we can attract something good and reverse the energy.

On this planet lessons are demanding, because on Earth as humans, we have forgotten what lies beyond the veil, and also the power we hold within. That makes us seem fragile and unprotected, but nothing is further from truth.

Keep in mind that we are not alone, and that help from beings of Light or other evolved consciousness, can always be called upon. At the same time, work on raising your energy levels, by adopting healthy habits.

CHAPTER 5

Raising an Individual Afflicted by Autism

Raising a child, whether with health issues or not, is one of the most noble things to do. But being a parent of a child with health issues, is one of the most demanding experiences a person can undertake. One must not forget, however, that we are souls having a human experience, so things need to be looked at from a different perspective or standpoint.

Many times, parents of children with health issues, tend to refer to themselves as parents with special children. They are looked on by society, either with awe for managing the challenge, or pitied for having a burden. Whatever the judgment, and the positive or negative charge, all opinions are ego-based, and fall under the energy of fear.

The truth is, that we are all souls on a journey and no one is above or below another.

Before reincarnation, all souls agree to assume a particular role. Children and parents as souls, agree on what experiences and lessons they want to undergo. All children and parents are equal, with none being of superior or inferior nature, to one another.

As you can see, nobody is "special" because each experience is important on its own. Judgments come from the ego and must therefore be put aside.

However, there is something else that we must bear in mind. All souls before reincarnation make contracts, but when we reach this planet, we forget everything that we agreed to previously. It is up to every single one of us, to reawaken and to recall our soul contracts.

When this is done, all in life is looked on from a different perspective. There prevails the energy of acceptance and of understanding alongside growth, whereas if we do not reawaken, there prevails pain and suffering, leading to separateness and grief.

As parents of autistic children, these issues come into play rather acutely on both sides, therefore the first thing these parents have to do, is work on themselves.

One of the biggest misleading concepts of parents, is to believe that they are separate from their child, and that they have to work on him or her. As parents of autistic individuals, you agreed on a soul level, to reawaken and to play a role in the raising of consciousness of humanity.

Your children are here to remind consciousness after consciousness, of this need and mission.

CHAPTER 6

Aloofness and Extreme Sensitivity

One of the characteristics often attributed to autism is aloofness. For many years, autism has been based on the misconception, that people afflicted by it, were closed in their own bubbles, and completely unaware of all that surrounds them.

Let me tell you that this couldn't be further from truth. It is quite the outer appearance that leads the rational mind to that conclusion.

While aloofness may seem apparent in autism, it is rather quite the opposite. Souls that agreed to reincarnate on this planet called Earth, are mostly old souls who agreed to reincarnate with autism, to help with the awakening of humankind, and to raise individual and collective consciousness.

And how do they do that, you may ask?

By doing the work, one soul at a time, beginning within every household, more specifically with parents.

Children with autism are here to remind mothers and fathers, who forgot, what was agreed to on a soul level. Some mothers and fathers are too attached to programming, where they function exclusively on what their senses perceive, and what their rational minds conclude, that the child is left on his/her own, living forever on this plane, with the energy of oddness and separateness.

The aloofness persists, not because the child does not feel, but rather because the pain and grief are so intense, he has to develop a barrier of self-protection against the hurt he feels and senses.

There are, however, households in which one of the parents is more sensitive and reawakens. In this case, the couple tends to deviate and separate, because the energy that brought them together is no longer there. In this situation, the child normally stays with the mother, coming to find more peace in the new home. If the mother is sensitive and eager to reach the child, she will soon find out that the best way is to work on herself and raise her vibration.

Autistic individuals are highly sensitive on many levels. They may have food sensitivities and great vulnerability to technology and electromagnetic frequencies. Their bodies which are highly vulnerable, very soon become burdened with toxicity, both from the environment and thought forms, which they pick up everywhere they go.

Let me explain this latter bit, so that you can understand clearly what is at play here.

Can you imagine yourself in a room full of people, who see you not for what you actually are, but for what they take you to be? They all speak the same language and because you are unable to speak it, they take it as truth that you don't understand it, because you may exhibit some peculiar traits or patterns of behavior they find odd.

They deviate from you either wanting to keep distance or because they believe you are unable to cross the bridge of communication. They begin, therefore, to talk about what interests them, forgetting about you or talking about you as if you simply are not there.

This is picked up by autistic individuals' sensitive, gigantic antennae and everything is heard at a very high pitch. It may become almost intolerable to bear both the sound, and what is said and unsaid.

Everything is picked up, and the grief and pain felt by autistic individuals, can lead to outbursts on the outside, but also to the development of toxins inside the body, and an even more fragile immune system.

When, however, the autistic individual's environment has a raised vibration, autistic individuals do not feel the world as such a menace, and this leads them to wish to step out of their bubble.

Aloofness is the need that autistic individuals have to be able to survive, when there is low vibrational energy in their environment, and the urge within to connect to the Divine.

When I was a young boy, many times I did not have the bubble of aloofness set, but that does not mean necessarily, that I wanted to be on this planet. In fact, one thing that pervades my memories is how painful it felt to be here.

As souls, we make decisions as to the experiences we want to undergo on Earth for our evolution, but when we cross the veil, we tend to forget. I say *tend* because not all forget completely.

Many autistic individuals have some memories quite present because of their unwillingness to be fully here, when the vibration is low in their surroundings.

At the same time, the fact that many people find them difficult to reach, leads many to resist being formatted or programmed by society. This, however, does not necessarily ease their path, because being able to sense, see and know what others cannot, is not easy.

As a young boy, and aware of my soul mission, I struggled a lot because I did not see space to be heard or understood, in my environment. In fact, for quite some time, I wanted to leave this planet, for I did not envision the possibility of change, which would work in my favor. All that I saw around me were rational thinkers, unable to question what they saw.

The amount of people who are absolutely dormant is astounding, and they bring pain upon themselves and those around them. It is therefore quite understandable that so many children with autism decide to remain aloof.

The world they see and sense around them is such a menace, with so much lack of understanding and openness to modify beliefs held as truth, that creating one's bubble of defense is the only way out.

The bubble keeps people away at large, and helps the individual seek solace in his connection to the Divine, which manages to remain untouched, because he is not too prone to programming.

Autism and its physical challenges have pressed hard times on me, but people turning their backs on me many times, has helped me to remain close to my connection to the Divine. It is the same for so many individuals.

Fortunately, my mother was sensitive enough to feel that I knew quite a lot more, than what the doctors and teachers were telling her, and that I could overcome my challenges. She continued to listen to her heart and intuition, and continued to bet on me. Although she often says this path also brought much pain, for she was left alone with me for some time.

My writing, although representing a window to my inner world, was different in nature, largely because of its spiritual content, which she could not understand.

She became divided between the happiness of having me express my thoughts, and the content of what was demanded to be said. It is this quest, that led her on a search of self-development, which helped both me and her. As she brought changes to her belief system, and brought herself closer to her Divine nature, she raised her vibration and brought us closer.

This is what needs to be done if parents of children with autism want to create a close relationship.

CHAPTER 7

Behaviors: Tip-toeing, Screaming and Repetition

TIP-TOEING

L inked to the characteristic of aloofness, many times present in autism, is the feature of tip-toe-ing.

What many see as a defect or weird walking, goes far beyond what the eyes can see.

As well as aloofness, tiptoeing is the autistic individual's means of expression, that the Earth plane is too dense for his/her sensitivity. The body has difficulty in taking in the energy from Earth, because of the density of the surrounding environment, and the belief systems based on fear.

The soul does not want to be fully grounded. In this case, it is not an energy bubble around the individual like aloofness, but extreme pain on the part of an autistic individual, which keeps him from being fully grounded.

As long as significant changes are not brought about, this feature will remain.

Some individuals may not tip-toe, or not have this as a marked feature like me, but may express this in another manner.

When I was young, whenever my mother told me to remove my shoes, I always had to fight against this idea, because the energy of the soil was too hard and painful on my body.

It took quite some time until I finally managed, but it did take time. Only when significant changes occurred at home, in terms of accepting what my mission was and raising vibration, did I manage to tread or walk on grass or sand.

The children who display autistic traits do it for a wide number of reasons. Many of them have got to do with the need to survive, on a heavily threatening planet.

SCREAMING

Screaming in autism is another very inconvenient feature, which I want to talk about. Very often people complain about it, but fail to accept completely, what is really behind it. Let me explain.

As I already mentioned, many autistic individuals easily connect with the Divine, because they have been left untouched, most of their lives, and therefore have not been formatted or programmed.

This has led them to constantly seek refuge in their soul, and also energy in other planes of existence. We do not exist solely on the Earth plane, but this plane is surely very demanding in terms of pain and the energy of fear.

Many individuals have lost connection with their soul, because of the formatting they have been exposed to through social media and archaic belief systems. This has led many people to lose the power of questioning, and to accept that fearful beliefs are part of their reality, disregarding the fact, that the only true energy is that of Love, and therefore of abundance and harmony.

When the energy of Love is imbalanced, then fear settles in. If this energy is left untreated, it will grow and take up space, consuming light on its way.

Autistic individuals, with their sensitive antennae, pick up on the energy of fear, chaos and tremendous pain, and the effect is excruciating. This leaves them with the one and only option left for them, and that is to scream.

They scream because of all the stimuli around them, picking up on the negative thought forms of their family, friends and neighbors. As they do so, they scream and try to tune into a higher frequency.

There is a massive collective consciousness full of hate, pain and chaos, and screaming is the only way to soothe the pain, and shake off the anger.

REPETITION

When it comes to autism, repetitive behavior seems to emerge and take its place right in the forefront, but what exactly is behind this behavior, and why does it occur?

We all know there are sensory issues in autism that lead to repetitive behavior. It can be caused by outside stimuli, and in order to protect ourselves we focus our minds on something else.

The way we try to continuously preserve ourselves, is done in a wide variety of manners. It can appear devastating to the innocent observer. In some instances, we repeat sounds or noises, and however annoying it may sound, it calms the body organically. The sound repetitions function as sound meditation on the brain, and a soothing feeling within is felt.

Most people do not understand this and tend to tell the person to keep quiet. Or they see the behavior as a means for the autistic individual to communicate something he wants. This attitude often leads to frustration on both sides.

On the one hand, the child or autistic person just wants to get control over a situation, and doesn't want to be told to shut down. On the other hand, the adult who does not know this, starts feeling frustrated or tense, because of the inability to understand what the individual is communicating.

The lack of understanding on both sides, often leads to clashes that could be avoided, if there was understanding of what was really going on. The repetitive behavior can assume other means of expression, for instance rocking to and fro, or even jumping.

In all these cases, it is important to understand the need that the autistic individual has to soothe discomfort or pain. The best thing to do in these cases, is to empty the mind of judgment and just let the person or child with autism be.

The behavior will fade, as soon as calmness returns to the stressed body.

CHAPTER 8

Energetic Issues and Seizures

ENERGY

Autism is not only a different way of viewing the world, and of sensing it, but also a neurological disorder derived from hyper-sensitivity to the environment. We also have an elevated amount of toxicity accumulated in the body, therefore the need to detoxify and to ensure clean eating.

There are however other issues coming into play, and that has to do with energetic issues. Let me explain.

Many individuals with autism are souls, with soul contracts to present themselves with the features of autism, to evolve as souls and release karma, but also to help humanity on planet Earth to awaken and ascend.

When we reincarnate and cross the veil, we forget most of what we agreed, as part of our soul contract with other souls.

Many individuals with autism however, because of their characteristics, manage to avoid constant programming and formatting by society, and they manage to keep connection to the Divine very active through their crown chakra.

In fact, this energy center of the body manages to remain very active for another reason. The souls who reincarnated with autistic traits, feel the energy of this planet so dense, with so much pain and chaos, that they fail to ground themselves fully on the planet, unless changes are brought about in the family unit, and society in general.

Everything for individuals with autism is felt intensely, and integrating into a normal life with strict routines and rules, can be very challenging. On the one hand, there is the need to integrate and become an integral part of society. On the other hand, there are all the menaces felt by the individual, such as lack of understanding and tolerance, and also sounds, lights and touch, that are felt and experienced at times with excruciating pain.

In the context of such experiences, and the demand to conform to a particular context, with a particular behavior, the person with autism may respond, out of fear and extreme pain, either by fighting what is sensed as threat, or fleeing in order to get free.

Whatever the situation at hand, fighting or fleeing, fear and anxiety are at the basis of the behavior.

SEIZURES

As most of you know, seizures are very common in autism. Physically there are reasons for their emergence, such as a predominantly toxic body, loaded with heavy metals, but also burdened with parasites, that silently breed in the body.

When we look into any kind of illness or disorder, we have to go deeper than the symptom. Besides the heavy metals and parasites, stress is another trigger, caused by emotions which are locked up in the emotional body.

Many autistic individuals are not accepted by their families and society as having increased sensitivity, and therefore their needs are not catered to.

Many times, individuals with autism have to endure contexts and situations, where people talk about them as if they weren't present, or simply do not understand a single word of what is being said.

Having difficulties of expression, especially when it comes to non-verbal autism, doesn't go hand in hand with difficulties of comprehension. The failure to acknowledge this, leads to feelings of rejection and non-acceptance in autistic individuals, as well as their will to not be fully grounded on this planet.

Most autistic individuals are very much connected to their inner being, and the energy of unconditional Love from other planes, where energy is more fluid and crystal clear. They sense the lack of Love on Earth, which leads them to reject the permanence on planet Earth.

They accumulate negative emotions and energy, which then fires and gives rise to seizures, in an attempt to break free from a burdened body, as well as a burdened existence.

CHAPTER 9

Communication

MISCOMMUNICATION

When it comes to autism, communication comes to the forefront. What do I mean?

One of the greatest challenges autistic individuals face, as well as their caretakers, is being able to bridge the issue of understanding of the two worlds. We have parents and caretakers with excessive focus on verbal expression, but communication goes far beyond the sound, and that has to be understood. Often the emphasis on spoken word is so much, that other cues on communication are overlooked.

The energy of parents and caretakers is of such tension, that individuals with autism can hardly look at the speakers, and instead of wanting to open up to the experience, prefer to shut down.

One of the things that has to be understood, is that humankind, despite having different languages, values oral communication. But they overlook things that are communicated subconsciously, and these things are picked up by autistic individuals.

Imagine having your vocal chords untouched, and wanting desperately to utter some sound, but the message does not get through from the brain. A message or command is given by the brain, but the body fails to respond.

The stress put on the individual is enormous, and tension tends to rise within. Now add another ingredient, and that is the disbelief by those around you (like a speech pathologist) that you can actually do it. There is a mismatch between what the person is asking you to do, and what she really believes you can do.

Because of this disbelief in your abilities, she may utter sounds (to prompt you to speak) but what is said is empty, and completely void of meaning. The sounds do not match the message, and communication cannot be established.

In fact, the miscommunication between individuals with autism and others, hurts deeply in the heart of those with non-verbal autism.

Before working on autistic individuals, parents and professionals should work on themselves and their belief system regarding autism. By that, I mean listening and reading what individuals with autism have been saying or writing about themselves.

There is often a huge gap between what is thought about autism, on the part of onlookers and people who are afflicted by the disorder.

A TWO-WAY STREET

A lot is said and written about autism and communication impairments, but much of what is said is a restricted and logical view, which does not provide a clear picture of what is really going on.

Autistic individuals are souls who incarnated with specific missions of contributing towards the evolution of humanity, and so many have not yet grasped the idea fully, and continue to impose old methods of communication solely based on speech or the written word.

It is true that although outdated, their importance is still huge and overwhelming, therefore I still put energy in getting my word across through writing, but there is the need to look deeper into the issue, if the great part of the population wants to really connect with individuals on the spectrum.

As I have said before, autistic individuals are not fully in their physical bodies, and they are still very much in touch with higher realms and dimensions, therefore they have a lot to share and teach.

It is urgent to put as much effort of communication skills on parents, caregivers and teachers and their ability of communicating through telepathy, as it is of mainstream forms of education on individuals with autism.

Unless the two-way road of communication is established, the messages going to and fro are a meager fraction, and changes on both sides will be too.

CHAPTER 10

Children of Today

The children of today are born with different characteristics from those of the past, and many times we do not recognize these differences, and children lose their potential.

These children have frail bodies, and the light in their hearts has difficulty surviving in the dense surrounding world.

They live in homes with parents disconnected from Source, from themselves, and from one another. These parents feed themselves with the type of home they own, the car they drive, and their professional success, and focus on schedules and bills to be paid.

Technology is another reality that drifts family members apart, and although they may be together they are very much apart. Besides the family environment, the children of today face difficulties of adapting to society in general.

BIRTH

I would like to talk about health care at birth. When a child is born, immediate contact between mother and child is not totally promoted, because the mother is sedated, and health professionals are busy with clinical procedures that they think are necessary to the baby. They forget that the physical contact between mother and child is crucial and that the love hormone oxytocin is released, reinforcing the ties of affection.

Immediately after birth an intense vaccine protocol follows, and the frail physical bodies and fragile immune systems collapse. Keep in mind that what may be good for one person, may be poison for another.

HEALTH CARE

Modern medicine has undoubtedly brought many benefits, but there is the need to rethink many aspects. The human being is a complex being with a lot of alchemy, energy and subtle bodies, which are compromised in a variety of ways. Therefore, reducing an individual to a symptom, and trying to solve things strictly through the use of a pill is, in my point of view, a simplistic way of looking at things.

The children of today need differentiated health care. The world has evolved and so has humanity. It is urgent to adjust health care and education to this evolution, because the distance between the real needs of the human being, and the solutions which are currently provided is enormous, and there is a lack of contribution to the development of the human being as a thinker and critic.

SCHOOLS

Let's take a look at education. Currently it is still very much dependent on memorization, and it does not stimulate the individual to create knowledge. It caters to the path of non-evolution and dependency, impeding the evolution of knowledge.

If we continue drinking water from the same fountain, just because its water was once drinkable and cleared our thirst, not paying attention to the fact that it has now become toxic, we will not be able to gather the real benefits of water. So it is, when it comes to education.

The children of today are born with a lot of sensitivity, and they do not conform to cold classrooms with lined up desks, where out-of-date or archaic knowledge is spilled out, with little utility in life.

The diseases that currently affect the majority of children, have a lot of do with modes of doing and being that are imposed upon them, and have nothing to do with their real needs or desires.

The children of today, the new humanity, bring forth a lot of knowledge, which did not occur in previous generations. Their consciousness is more awake and many of them share knowledge with the adults.

When they have the misfortune of having parents and other adults that are still not awake, they see their future conditioned, and they feel sad. There are also a lot of children who are fidgety and medicated. During their adolescence, they may revolt against their family and society, and they are labeled as rebellious.

At school, they are not very successful and they are diagnosed as having learning difficulties and attention deficit disorder. These students and adolescents transform into adults with low self-esteem and easily become depressed. The truth is that humanity is very distracted and is not aware of its self-destruction.

The conditioning of humanity begins early in life. When we reincarnate, we receive in our early infancy, energy which is not ours and beliefs that nobody questions. This essentially serves to program or format individuals, in order to behave as sheep of the same flock.

Children hear comments about themselves in their early days, that do not correspond to truth, but because people insist on them, they take them as absolute truths.

How does this work then?

For example, when a child goes to nursery school and she has a meltdown, nobody questions the real cause of the behavior, and opt to call her a spoiled child. Of course, you might say that meltdowns are a part of childhood, and a way of marking territory, but I alert you towards the way that we often react towards this type of behavior. The reaction may not be appropriate because the child may be in pain, or even seeing things that make her feel afraid, but nobody assumes that possibility.

Children have always had visions, but their parents, from the very beginning, have made them believe that it is part of their imagination. Parents are unable to understand that they make their children fragile with this type of attitude. They become insecure and their personal power is removed, and harm can be done throughout their lives, because they grow up doubting what they hear, see and feel.

Schools have a lot of weight when it comes to weakening human beings. The fact that children continue to be labeled because of their failure at school, provokes in them beliefs of incapacity.

The teachers who follow archaic teaching methods of the era of the industrial revolution, catalogue these children early on, as rebellious, lacking concentration, and having learning disabilities. They do this on account of a pseudo-objectivity, that the education system imposed upon themselves too.

Teachers themselves are the product of normalization, therefore they reproduce this behavior. They forget that the human being is complex and marvelous, and they hinder the minds of children, whose learning needs do not match the great need of memorization. These children become passive subjects in the construction of knowledge.

Children suffer from an early age from the need to categorize, the intelligent and the not so intelligent. The first are very successful at school, therefore, their personal power is strengthened in all areas of life. The latter are not less intelligent, but start to protect themselves and pick up on the beliefs of others, that they are less worthy. These beliefs have repercussions in their private and professional life for a very long time.

What happens is that Love, which ought to be the moving force in the human being, is locked out from children's hearts, and they lose focus of themselves and of others.

SPECIAL KIDS

I want to share more information about children with special characteristics that keep coming onto our planet.

It is more common to hear about children who have special gifts which surface at an early age, or that arrive on Earth suffering from autism.

When it comes to autism there are a lot of factors contributing to its development, whether these factors have to do with genetics, high rates of toxicity in our environment, water and food or even gastrointestinal issues.

If you take a look around you will notice that the number of children suffering from autism is rising. I would like to tell you that autism is on our planet with the clear mission of inviting humanity to awaken.

The souls that agreed to come to planet Earth with autism, and to face its challenges, want to help humanity gain consciousness of the need to go back to authenticity, to what is genuine and to respect nature.

Non-verbal individuals with autism, we should say, fear the state of the planet, and unless they feel that their surrounding environment and their family are willing to awaken, the compromise they made with their soul becomes very demanding.

Non-verbal autism starts with the challenge of communication between the individual that presents autistic traits, and his family. There is an obstacle to be overcome between the autistic individual and his environment. The individual with non-verbal autism communicates tele-pathically and subtly, and only people who are sensitive enough, will be able to communicate with and understand him/her.

Autistic individuals who are non-verbal are connected with other dimensions and planes where communication is very different from what it is on planet Earth. Despite the efforts that may be made with the intention of promoting or developing speech, the efforts will prove themselves worthless, because the autistic individual does not see a reason to communicate the way it is intended.

The way to obtain that result, is by parents raising their energy and allowing the autistic child to fully reincarnate. When parents, teachers and therapists who work with the autistic child change their field of vibration, and rise in terms of frequency, the autistic individual is touched and yields to come closer to life on Earth.

THE ERA OF AQUARIUS

I wish to draw your attention to a spiritual issue behind the challenges that we are forced to face in life. Autism is one of them, and the more severe it is, the greater the invitation for a reflection on spiritual issues.

Autism aims at drawing humanity's attention towards the path it has taken throughout time, and its mode of being on this planet. It intends to draw people's attention towards the air, nutrition and relationships, making them more transparent and genuine.

The autistic individual responds to the need of humanity to regain its strong inner power, which has become very dormant. The era of Pisces, before the era of Aquarius, which we are now in, brought us individualization, or rather the deviation of humanity from its essence, and a turning to materialism and superficiality.

In that phase of industrial and economic development, the individual centered himself more in having, rather than in being. Both men and women disconnected from themselves and one another. Putting the emphasis on the outside, they misled themselves, thinking that power has to do with the amount of material things.

In the era of Aquarius there is an appeal to being.

The common human being acts according to his logical mind, and his limited perspective of his sight range. But the real power does not lie in the logical mind, therefore the world is in chaos.

Throughout the years, there has been technological and material advancement, but there is still a lot to uncover regarding the essence of humanity, and so the feeling of emptiness is installed. Autism intends to awaken in humanity, the interest in that part of itself, that has been forgotten.

Looking at autism in a rational perspective, we conclude that the individual has a disability, and we cover him/her with the veil of death or loss of hope. However, if there is space to listen to the inner voice, and look with the power of the third eye and intuition, the result can be surprising.

As I said before the individual with autism, especially if he is non-verbal, has his soul caught in other planes and does not accept reincarnation, unless there are changes especially in the family unit, and those that surround him.

The soul of the autistic individual proposed with a new reincarnation, to help with the awakening of humanity, and the raising of its vibration and frequency level. Humanity, however, is dormant and the planet suffers with ongoing pain and terrorism. Although the amount of souls that volunteer to come back to Earth and help with its ascension is increasing, the truth is that humanity is largely dormant and castration continues.

RESPECTING THE PLANET

Our planet at the moment is crying out the pleas of Mother Earth, so that there is respect for the planet and all forms of life. The natural balance was shaken, and greed and corruption has taken over humanity. Everything comes together with a price, and humanity with its forgetfulness of its true essence, has brought high costs, being swallowed by the forces of the energy of revenge and lack of pity.

The planet does do not ask for us to save it, but rather to take care of ourselves. Throughout times, the human being has looked to the outside, when the key to it all, is to look inside. The moment that humanity looks inside and takes care of balance, everything around it will change.

When we are in balance and feeling well with ourselves, we become stronger, and do not allow sickness to install in, or around us. When we are in balance, we do not cause pain around us and we respect our surrounding environment. Therefore, the plea to save the planet is deceiving, because each and every one of us, can only save one person, him or herself.

The planet and all that surrounds it, corresponds to our vibration and what we constantly think. When our surrounding energy and that of ourselves, is dense with conflict or rage, the events and happenings we attract, are of that nature and we all suffer.

There is collective energy and individual energy, but each can produce personal changes within, because these will come through in collective changes. Planet Earth will thank every human being who takes care of his or her energy, because a greater harmony will be achieved this way.

The increase of autism is also linked to a high level of toxicity on this planet. Although the people who are autistic are viewed as having a disability, the souls that proposed to reincarnate as such, volunteered to come forth this way to begin changes on planet Earth, and it all begins at home.

I would like to share with you that it is urgent for humanity to awaken soon, and autism spreads throughout the world with this function. It is necessary to learn more about it, and listen to what your heart tells you about it, so that great advances can be brought about on Earth.

Besides people with autism, there are other souls that arrive on planet Earth with the mission of helping humanity remember the eternity of its consciousness, and the fact that we are not only physical bodies.

The children of today present characteristics that others born in previous decades, did not reveal in such an evident way. I would like to refer to their high sensitivity to all that surrounds them, therefore many suffer from food allergies, hay fever and even asthma. Their bodies are exposed to toxic environments, but also to collective modes of thinking.

The number of people that do not know that the visible has great influence on the invisible and collective, is astounding. The only solution is to educate the masses, explaining that we are much more than the physical body, and that we are all linked to one another.

After taking into account this phenomenon, the first step is for everyone to work on themselves, adopting healthy living habits and completely altering their modes of thinking.

The world changes one consciousness at a time, because the most subtle change affects the whole.

SECTION III

JOÃO ANSWERS PARENTS' QUESTIONS

Introduction

One of the most powerful things I can do for parents, is to give them a new understanding of their children. While my own journey has led me to many conclusions and solutions, none are as powerful as the questions and answers that follow.

João taps into another realm, that I have not practiced, nor do I know how to reach at present. He is remarkable and candid at honing in on the real issues at hand, so parents do not have to wonder and second guess what they are doing.

As I have read, and reread these pages many times, I am always brought back to the most important thing that I can do for *my* child – to work on myself first. It is not an easy command. Quite the contrary, it is some of the hardest work I know. But nevertheless, if we want our children to thrive, we have to set the stage for them to thrive and that begins with our own inner work.

I hope you gleam useful advice from João's words as I have. It is his dream to be a Soul doctor, and I hope you will agree that he is well on his way. I am so grateful to be sharing his wisdom here with you, so that your journey becomes a more peaceful and loving process.

The questions that follow were submitted by parents looking for answers to help their own children.

CHAPTER 11

Communication

How can I help my 25-year old son communicate more effectively?

My 25-year old son struggles to use sign language, augmentative communication (TouchChat on iPad), Rapid Prompting Method and typing. As his communication partner and mother, I struggle to understand his answers to open ended questions on the letter board.

How can I help my son communicate more effectively?

My son is so intelligent and I want so desperately to communicate effectively with him.

Dear Mom,

Thank you for writing and let me start by telling you that being desperate does not do any of you any good. You are pushing and pushing but the more you push the more resistance you will face.

Individuals with autism are souls who reincarnated with the mission of awakening humanity and have no wish to be totally grounded, as long as the appropriate conditions have not been met, and one of them is acceptance of what is, and having families relearning to communicate.

Oral and written expression are important but have led people to put their attention outward.

It is important to relearn to look inward and practice listening to our inner voice, at the same time visualizing people who we want to reach, and sending love, and telling them what is in our heart.

If you surrender, you will open space to hear your son telepathically and when you do this, and he feels you no longer push, he will adhere to communicating as you wish, whether through a letter board or any other method he feels appropriate.

Blessings,
João Carlos

How can I get my 11-year old son more motivated to communicate with RPM (Rapid Prompting Method)?

I have an 11-year old son with autism and he is non-verbal. We have been using RPM to facilitate communication but he seems resistant and not very motivated.

How can I get my son to be more motivated to do RPM, and also to become more fluid and skilled at it? I would love to know how we can make the experience more motivating for others too.

Dear Mom,

Let me start by telling you something in regard to your question on how to help your son. First of all, it is important to take into account tremendously, the type of beings we are dealing with.

Unlike what humanity has been used to, individuals with autism favor other types of communication, like telepathy, and not oral or written expression, which is what most people do.

Autistic individuals are souls which incarnated with the purpose of raising up humanity - through the bridging of differences and awakening. That being said, your son will not feel motivated to communicate through RPM, or any other means, solely on your terms or what has persisted throughout time.

The first step is for you to work on acceptance that he may not be fully motivated now, and join him in his singular form of communication. Join him in his stimming or other behaviors with childlike playfulness and without judgement. Make him feel at ease and not constrained, and when he feels this loving space without imposition or expectation, he will open up and give hands to bridge his world and yours.

Only then will he feel the want and need to find a means to get his word out, be it spoken or typed, RPM or facilitated communication.

Blessings,
João Carlos

(Further question from mom for clarity on previous question)

It is really hard for me to accept things the way they are because I am afraid my son will not progress. Can you help me understand acceptance better? And also, is the school he attends, a good school?

Dear Mom,

First there has to be changes of perception on your regard, as to making your son want to communicate on your terms.

When it comes to autism, imposition and obliging leads to frustration on all sides. As we go along and feel acceptance, instead of pushing, we tend to open up. We become more receptive and eager to communicate, in a manner that most people on the spectrum are not used to.

Let's turn things around. How do you think your son feels about his needs, or mode of communication, not being met? The frustration you feel with his poor adherence to RPM or FC, is the same that he feels, in your not wanting to become more telepathic and intuitive.

Autism is on the rise and it is not solely due to environmental factors. It is also a wake-up call to humanity, to change lifestyle and to awaken, and look inside to regain power through intuition and vibration.

Humans need to increase their frequency and vibration, and when they do, autistic souls will be more accessible and grounded.

Changes become more noticeable, when the vibration within families, matches the vibration of the autistic individual they are trying to help.

It is a good school that your son attends, but what I told you to work on, also applies to his teachers.

Blessings,
João Carlos

How do we get past objections to communicate, in my minimally verbal son, because it's "too hard"?

My teenage son with autism has minimal language. He can tell you what he wants or where he wants to go, or make a one or two-word comment about something. He can also ask simple questions like "what's for dinner?" Most of his sentences are limited to a few words.

We cannot have conversations that go back and forth between us. Because of this I do not have any idea what is really going on inside his head. We try asking him questions that are very simple, but he often objects and says "No! Too hard!"

If we keep pushing it will escalate into a tantrum. Can you tell me why he objects?

Dear Mom,

Here are my insights in regards to your son. Your son seems to object to giving some answers, but this is not always true. Sometimes we do not answer because of the struggle we have, in having our brain give commands, which are not followed by our body.

Other times, we feel that low expectations are held in regard to us, so we do not feel motivated. Another aspect is that people are not ready to hear what we have to say, so we close down.

Work on leaving space for your son to find his timing, and you will be impressed.

Blessings,
João Carlos

How can we communicate with our 5-year old grandson who is non-verbal with autism?

I am the grandmother to a 5-year old boy with autism. His communication skills are so limited, and he has sensory processing disorder.

I am a health coach, but have had minimal success with positive changes. It is so frustrating as he is about to enter public kindergarten.

We have tried all we know, but still can't communicate with our precious grandson. What can we do?

I also wonder if there is there a genetic or past generation issue we need to address?

Any recommendations you have would be greatly appreciated and whole heartedly received. We desire the ability to communicate with our grandson, and to see him flourish as the sweet little boy he is!

Dear Grandmother,

Your grandson is a child with telepathic means of communication. Nowadays there is a significant number of children who are highly sensitive, and are very much in touch with their soul or Higher Self. For them speech is not necessary to communicate, because they communicate telepathically and pick up on people's thoughts.

I suggest not putting so much stress on verbal communication, so as not to create tension, and seek out ways of improving the family's belief systems and thought forms linked to your grandson's speech.

When this aspect loses the heightened focus it has, the family will make a quantum jump in their sensitivity, and be able to connect to him telepathically, and he will be more available to try and connect through speech.

Yes, there is a past generation issue to address linked to communication, or rather miscommunication. Your grandson has come forth with this issue for all those around him, especially family, to learn to communicate based on the energy of Love and acceptance, and not on demand.

Love and light,
João Carlos

CHAPTER 12

Behaviors

Why does my 12-year old son move around constantly - jumping, twisting, vocalizing and more?

My son is in almost constant motion, except when he is really focused. He is either vocalizing, making sounds, rocking, squeezing his hands together, twisting his shirt, jumping, inhaling sharply, turning his neck, touching his genitals, covering his ears or grinding his teeth. And he likes to listen to music or videos on a high volume.

Why is his body constantly moving? Is there anything I can do to help him calm his body so he can function better?

Dear Mom,

Let me give you some insight about what is going on with your son.

As we all know individuals with autism have sensory issues. Some however are on the severe side, and this is something that is affecting your son. But there are other issues.

Part of the sensory issues are from a physical body which is burdened with heavy metals, causing brain inflammation and therefore alterations in terms of behavior and wellbeing. We feel excruciating pain, or a body dumbed with stiffness, and we feel compelled to jump, scream or bite even, to get out of this situation affecting our body.

This is the physical and rational perspective, but we have to go beyond that and see the spiritual aspect, too. On this issue, your son is a soul like so many others that volunteered to come to this planet and third dimension. But on arrival, and feeling the density of duality, he has not fully embodied or grounded, and will refuse to do so as long as he does not feel safe, and the people around him are not behaving on the frequency of Love, and therefore non-judgmental.

Join your son in his behaviors with childlike playfulness, and then space occurs for him to join you in the way most people require.

Blessings,
João Carlos

Why is my 12-year old son having such difficulties sleeping?

My son's sleeping is not good. He wants to sleep in my bed and I or my husband end up sleeping in his little bed. He wakes up during the night and makes a lot of noise. It's hard to sleep even if he is in another room.

Why is he having such difficulties? I have tried homeopathy to help with this and other issues, but I am curious to know what you feel is going on?

Dear Mom,

You are blessed and very much loved. As for the sleeping issues, individuals with autism are often empaths and pick up on stagnant energy and limiting thought patterns, and also energy of fear.

Clean your home energetically and all your energy fields. If you feel it, play the mantras OM and Om Mani Padme UM.

Let go of the ego because the ego is based on fear and Source is Infinite Love.

Blessings,
João Carlos

Why does my highly sensitive 13-year old daughter have bursts of energy in the evenings?

My children have not been diagnosed as being on the spectrum, but they are both highly sensitive. I have a question about my 13-year old daughter, and was hoping you could shed some light.

My 13-year old daughter who is highly sensitive, has bursts of energy in the evenings, and I have been trying to figure out the pattern to learn the trigger, and hopefully discover the root cause. In the evenings, she has to physically move her body, and does things like jump around, doing her cheerleading moves (such as the splits or high kicks). When she was younger, she would flop around on the bed excessively.

I would be grateful for any insight that can help me support her and whatever may be going on.

Dear Mom,

Thank you for your question and I do not restrict to answering questions on autism. We are One and part of the Whole that is, therefore there are no drawers of them and us.

Your daughter is a highly sensitive child like so many more that are spread throughout the world, yet people continue to view children with a lens of the past and being blind to the changes that these newly arrived souls are here to teach and show.

Children nowadays are very much connected to their Inner Being and Source and have trouble behaving and conforming to patterns of former children.

Your daughter is like a sponge and picks up energy and thought patterns that are stagnant or blocked and she needs to shake this energy off her auric field. It is important for her to be in contact with nature, going for walks in parks or at the seaside to ground and release energy that does not serve her wellbeing.

Blessings,
João Carlos

CHAPTER 13

Independence

How can I find meaningful direction for my 14-year old son with autism?

My son is very bright, but he still has many challenges to overcome. I worry about his future and wonder how we can take his talents and turn them into meaningful work. I'm not sure how to help him with the right direction so he can enjoy work as an adult?

Dear Mom,

First of all, in regard to your son, it is important to say that as souls, we do not come with a guidebook. Although there are soul contracts before birth, when on Earth not all souls, because of inappropriate conditions or free will choices, do not manage to accomplish their missions.

Your son is a sensitive boy who has challenges, but his first aim as a soul, is to get his family awake and conscious, that there is more to what is, than what the eye can see. A lot of what we see, is built on personal vibration and frequency. Therefore, what you believe about your son, is going to influence how far he will get to be.

If you work on yourself every day, and allow all of your children to live in a space of Love, and believe that your son has innate wisdom, which will show in due timing, you will get a son that is grounded and overcoming what you thought impossible.

Blessings,
João Carlos

What can I do to support my twins with autism, to make life on Earth easy, fulfilling and pleasant?

I have 9-year old twins with autism, a girl and a boy. I would like to know how I can I help my children become the best self they can be in this life time?

I would also like to know what I can do to support them and make life on Earth easy, fulfilling and pleasant?

Dear Mom,

Let me begin by telling you that we cannot, contrary to popular belief, provoke change on others directly.

Each and every one can only bring about change within himself, and as one does so, our energy alters and our vibration and frequency changes.

This leads to changes in all and everyone around us, for when we speak of energy and vibration, like attracts like. When we work on ourselves, cater to our body, and well-being of mind, body and spirit, everyone is affected because we are all One.

I guess this isn't what you were expecting as an answer, but the truth is, if you want your children to be happy, or have a fulfilling life, start being happy and create space for personal growth and fulfillment.

Your children will sense the energy, and changes will be a short distance from themselves.

Give out what you wish for and it will come back to you twofold.

Blessings,
João Carlos

What either physical or spiritual, is my son's biggest block to being neurotypical?

I have 16-year old and 14-year old sons with autism. I would like to know what the blocks are that are keeping my sons from being neurotypical? And what can I do to clear these blocks?

Dear Mom,

First of all, let me start by telling you that both your sons, as souls, proposed to come forth as autistic and not as neurotypical.

Of course, there are some physical issues to be addressed, but being autistic is not necessarily a feature that you outgrow.

There are reasons for coming forth with autism, and one of them is for the soul's evolution and of those around him. The best way to help your boys, is to start working on yourself. Remember that what we see in others exists within, so start clearing what you perceive in your boys. As you do so, you will change and ultimately provoke change, for we are all One.

Love and light,
João Carlos

Why did my son become autistic and how can I recover him?

My son is 9-years old and he has autism. I want to know how he became autistic. Was there something specific that happened to him?

I would like to know how to help him recover holistically. What do I need to focus on with regards to diet and holistic therapies?

Dear Mom,

First of all, let me tell you that things go deeper than the mind's eye can see. Whatever could have contributed to your son's autism, whether an environmental toxin or genetic predisposition, we have to understand there is a soul purpose, and soul contracts which are made before reincarnation.

We are consciousness or spiritual beings having physical experiences, so before the decision to be born on this dense Earth plane, each and every soul, in order to evolve, proposes a series of experiences, and together with other souls, contracts are made for the purpose of evolution. It was so with your son, as with each and every one of us.

Let me also tell you, that whatever the experience a soul decides to undergo, there is always the intention of evolution and growth of all those involved. Your son as a soul, agreed with those around him, to come forth with autistic features, for the evolution of all, including himself.

Autistic individual's recovery depends on many aspects, such as a clean diet and therapies, but also on the awakening of the souls of all those around them.

Love and light,
João Carlos

Will my 13-year old non-verbal son have an independent future?

I am very interested in João's personality because my 13-year-old son is somehow like him - low functioning non-verbal, but very intuitive. And I also imagine his future as an independent and happy man who helps people become conscious about gifts such kids give to all of us.

I would like to ask him about the future of my son. Will he speak verbally? Will he be able to graduate a school? Will music be his occupation (probably working with kids like himself)?

Dear Mom,

Thank you for writing and let me start by explaining a few things. When it comes to predictions it is not easy to give an answer for certain, because multiple things are at play. There are multiple or parallel realities, with different versions of ourselves and all outcomes are possible.

However, the one that comes visible in the third-dimension reality is dependent on free will choices, frequency and vibration.

Based on these issues and therefore your current energy, and of your son, if you do not shift tremendously in terms of decreasing your vibration, your son has high chances of overcoming his challenges and leading a fulfilling life.

Work on yourself and see in your heart a healthy and wholesome son.

Blessings,
João Carlos

Will my 15-year old son ever live independently?

Here are several questions I hope João can answer about my son.

Do you have any practical strategies to help my son tolerate or try Irlen glasses?

We keep hearing about how energies are shifting for these kids, but when will we, who don't pick up on energies so well, 'see' the shift? How might we experience it?

Will my son ever be able to live independently?

Does he want to go to school?

Has Joao continued with seizures or did he grow out of them?

Recently a trusted source for information for me, told me that where we live is driving my son crazy. She hasn't had time to elaborate but I'm wondering if João can corroborate her feelings? Obviously, we wouldn't be able to up and move immediately, but if it's something we need to plan for we'll look into it.

My wife wants to know if he will independently communicate with us in a way she can understand. I think it goes without saying that he is already communicating, right? But she's more of a left-brain type so wants some evidence he doesn't need prompting.

Dear Dad,

Blessings from above. First of all, and most important for you to understand, is that we are a whole lot more than a physical body, and even when it comes to the physical body there isn't a one-size fits all. We are all unique in some way, and so what might make a difference to one individual may not work for another.

But there is another thing that comes into play, and that is your intention or belief system. That being said, whatever it may be, when it comes to healing, if there isn't a mind, body, spirit connection, results will always be far from total satisfaction. That leads me to the answer of the first question.

My dear friend, what makes you think he may need Irlen glasses? Have you thought that perhaps he may not necessarily need them, and your ego is in the front seat here. I would suggest to remain calm in regards to this, and out of that place of calmness, introduce them a little at a time and without pushing.

The energy of children that keep arriving on this planet is different and will continue to be so. You will only be able to see a shift when you work on yourself, so that you will be a match. When it comes to energy, frequency and vibration, like attracts like. There is no other way to go about it.

As far as your son living independently it all comes down to the appropriate conditions being secured. By that I mean working on your belief system and raising self-awareness, in order to increase your vibration and less self-sabotage.

As for school, we also have to perceive what school is. Schooling serves the purpose of providing a context where an individual can acquire knowledge and construct knowledge, but it does not necessarily have to take place confined to the walls of mainstream education. This being said your son does want to grow and share wisdom, but he is not open to shutting down in a regular state or public school, so choose wisely.

When it comes to my seizures, they have come to reduce with the help of medication, which was necessary to implement because, despite them being energy activations, they were too strong and putting my body at risk.

Once again, we need to find balance, so medication at times can prove helpful in protecting our body from receiving too much energy, which is difficult for it to withstand. But even in these cases, caution has to be taken so as not to shut down the individual.

Your trusted friend is a great intuitive and has probably tuned into the energy of your neighborhood and the frequency of its vibration. Are the people totally rational thinkers and individualistic, valuing only the material or visible, or do they have openness to living more authentic lives?

There is also the issue of electromagnetic influence which has to be looked into. If too high the rate of electromagnetism, your son is subject to more strain on his sensitive body. Look into these issues.

As for your wife and a little on your part too, you are looking for all the answers outside yourselves, and you have come across very good pathways to help support your son. But there is a shift that is needed on your behalf, to shift from sole rational thinking, to a joint collaboration between heart and mind.

Your son is vibrating at the heart level and if you mind

vibrate exclusively, both your son and you won't meet changes.

Autism is here to shift outdated paradigms and every individual has free will choice, so you have to choose to grow, or to remain in third dimensional thought mode.

Blessings,
João Carlos

What are the most important aspects to include when creating an organization to serve autistic individuals with independence?

I am part of an organization that was started for the purpose of creating supportive housing opportunities for young adults on the autism spectrum.

As we begin developing our first project, I would greatly appreciate João's insights and knowledge of what services, assurances and best practices we should incorporate into our autism community.

Dear Friend,

First and foremost, thank you for your contact and the work you are doing to improve the lives of autistic individuals.

When it comes to helping the autism community certain

things are important to bear in mind. One of the most important has to do with the people who are going to work there or provide assistance. How do they see, feel and perceive autism? Is it a dead-end road or a way of perceiving the world in a different manner and raising consciousness?

Then location is very important. Nature has healing and soothing aspects that cannot be disregarded. The facilities have to take into account the needs of this community with good noise cutting infrastructures and the preoccupation to not make use of fluorescent lighting or any containing mercury.

Decrease also electromagnetic frequency, because all these things interfere with the delicate bodies of autistic individuals. Make sure there is water which is clean of chemicals, and energize it with mantras and reproduce Solfeggio sounds in the environment. These few actions act upon all individuals in the community, on the whole contributing to wellness and raising the vibration of space and people.

Another aspect to bear in mind is the need for sunshine and sea, because of their healing properties for all. Energy healing modalities are important as well, as is a good provider of organic farming. The food and its quality is crucial, but not less are those that handle and prepare it.

Animals are less evolved consciousness, but play a vital role in promoting wellbeing and strengthening ties between humankind and other living beings.

There is much to say, but I hope to have helped in giving this short contribution.

Best regards,
João Carlos

CHAPTER 14

Education

Is a mainstream classroom the best option for my 5-year old daughter?

My daughter is almost 5-years old and was diagnosed with ASD at age three. She has been progressing, thank God, but still struggles with anxiety symptoms and some auditory issues.

I am planning on mainstreaming her from an autistic school to a small private school. What are your intuitive thoughts on her and this decision?

Dear Mom,

It is good to come together and to share thoughts and insight. Your daughter is a beautiful little girl and very delicate.

More important than mainstreaming is to be aware of how she reacts to the people who surround her and work with her. It is not the place in itself that is going to make a difference but rather the energy and belief systems of the people that will work with her.

Do they accept that autism is another way to perceive the world or sense it, or are they formatted into fixing her and making her conform into normality?

These two attitudes will lead to different outcomes and will let you have a stronger and successful child who thrives on the energy of Love, or locks herself in great anxiety and frustration.

Feel with your heart.

Blessings,
João Carlos

Is my 17-year old severely autistic son ready to learn to read and write?

My son is 17-years old. When he was ten, he was diagnosed with severe autism and he is completely non-verbal. I would like to begin on a high note because he is indeed doing really well. He is in a home for special needs youth since 2015 and seems very happy there.

He has experienced a lot of trauma due to his regressive autism and my inability to fully understand the nature of his autism. We did intensive ABA for years and all the while he regressed. It was all too much for him.

My question to you is, does my son want to learn to read and write? I would like his school to try and teach him again. Do you think he is ready now?

Dear Mom,

Your son has indeed gone through challenging times and has indeed finally found some peace.

Non-verbal autistics have very challenging missions because they are here for the awakening of humanity. Unless changes occur, first among their families, they will refuse to get grounded and communicate in a way we would like them to.

In your son's case, like in so many, he will only accept reaching out, if it comes out of a place of Love, without instant or constant pressure, because there is a world within him ready to be shared.

Blessings,
João Carlos

I am creating a job training and employment organization for autistic individuals. What are your insights about this endeavor?

I have a 10-year old daughter on the spectrum. She is minimally verbal and a very smart cookie. I have always wanted a productive and beautiful future for her. With the current state of the world, she will not likely have a lot of opportunity to participate and contribute to her fullest potential.

I started an organization that provides job training and employment to people on the spectrum.

We are moving into our own workspace in June. It is an opportunity to create an innovative training and work center-- that can be a hub to introduce all others to our untapped and talented autistic workforce.

Please send along any thoughts you have -- anything at all that you think we should know, or be aware of, as we set out to create and develop this space. I would be grateful for your feedback and anything you would like to share with us.

Dear Mom,

As you say, your daughter is a very beautiful soul who has come forth to assist humankind in its ascension process. You yourself agreed before reincarnation to assist her in reaching her fullest potential, despite her challenges. You have so far, come a long way in preparing her pathway to success alongside others.

Your project answers the wishes of many autistic individuals and their families to be productive and included members of society. But it is important to point out that autistic individuals are very sensitive to energy and thought patterns, therefore it is of utter importance that you pay attention to this issue. Make sure your space is energetically clean and that everyone around takes care of having time to clean their energy fields.

When it comes to doing anything with autistic individuals there has to be trust, sensitivity and awareness because autism is a characteristic which empowers individuals to spot hypocrisy and falsehood.

Energy can empower when light and bright, so keep that in mind so that your daughter can then thrive. Do not exclude the energy of spaces.

Blessings,
João Carlos

What is the best option for a school for my 6-year old son with autism?

I would like to better understand my 6-year old son with autism. What are the best schooling options for him. And how do I find the best protocol for his health and wellness?

Dear Mom,

Your son is a child with high levels of sensitivity and most of his behavior has to do with his ability to pick up blocked energy and fearful beliefs.

Schools are places of stagnant energy, where children are formatted to conform to limiting beliefs. Children who are sensitive and live essentially on the energy of Love, have difficulty conforming to imposed stale beliefs, and therefore suffer.

They have to be balanced energetically, as well as their families. As a way to ease their pain, changes have to be brought about within the home setting, having their parents awaken, and following a diet that caters to wholesome food for the body.

Love and light,
João Carlos

CHAPTER 15

Aggression

Why does my 10-year old son become aggressive and refuse to communicate, and enjoy being treated like a baby?

I am teaching my 10-year old son to communicate through facilitated communication. I have the feeling that he doesn't want, or can't work with me.

Once he was working with an experienced therapist, he revealed that he didn't want to work and wanted to be treated as a baby.

Why isn't he motivated to improve his communication with me through FC?

When he gets upset, he sometimes scratches and hits. How can I help him to reduce his aggression?

Is there any sport or activity that you would recommend for my son to try?

Dear Mom,

First of all, let me start by telling you that communication in autism occurs in a variety of ways and not always as you may expect.

Your son is still not open to communicate in the way you might want him to and therefore reacts aggressively, expressing his frustration at not managing to express himself in the way he would like. He is frustrated at having things imposed, as if it will make him fit more concretely in society.

Your son wants to be like a baby because babies communicate and people can understand them, despite no verbal expression on their part.

Let that be your starting point with your son.

As for a sport, start off with hiking because it soothes the mind, besides doing wonders for the physical body.

As you calm down, so will your son.

Blessings,
João Carlos

How can I help my 14-year old son with severe aggression towards our family?

I am the mother of three boys, the youngest is 14-years old and has severe, non-verbal autism. I have been trying to help him for many years with many therapies. I know deep in myself, what a beautiful and wise soul he is, who cannot express his true essence due to the condition of his body.

But there is especially one huge barrier which makes things so much harder for him and us, and this is his aggression, which can be dangerous to everyone around. It is very unpredictable with episodes coming out of nowhere.

I thought this might be due to PANS/PANDAS, and I have been using a holistic approach for one month now. He is slowly getting better, with ups and downs, making the path challenging, but giving hope for improvement.

One very important issue that we need to heal is our family relations. My son cannot tolerate to be around his brothers. Their presence makes him react with aggressive gestures, which turn into aggressive attacks, if they don't go to their rooms. Most of the time his brothers are hiding, locked in their rooms.

It is an unbearable burden for us, and all my love and knowing who my son truly is, does not help me solve this situation.

Can you please help with insights on how to heal the situation? How can I help my son, his brothers, and my entire family?

Dear Mom,

First of all, blessings from Heaven and secondly, let me explain some issues you brought up.

Aggressiveness may come along with autism, although it is not necessarily a part of it.

The reason it appears, may be due to frustration, or a means to communicate, or simply a response to blocked or stagnant energy. It is not something that arrives from nowhere.

Your first attitude to help your son, is to find out under which category his explosions occur. If these episodes are frequent, try clearing your space with sage, and start observing your thought patterns or beliefs, and start working on them.

Your son is a sensitive teenager and as such, is able to pick up on fearful thought patterns and that does not help to connect the family.

As a first step to helping your son, work on yourself and him, by looking at him with a new perspective of wholesomeness, instead of needing fixing or fitting into conformity.

Blessings,
João Carlos

Why has my 14-year old son suddenly regressed and become very angry?

My 14-year old son has been progressing steadily until the last two to three months. He was learning in school, had minimal aides help, and even joined wrestling. Now, he is seeing people in his imagination and yelling at them. He is swearing a lot and snapping his fingers to cope.

He is very angry and never used to be this way. He says some characters are trying to hurt him and his friends and his toys.

We changed his diet to a holistic protocol last month. We have tried supplements and homeopathy, but his behaviors seem to be increasing.

I just want to help him get back to being happy and moving forward. I feel like he also feels helpless. He says characters are ruining his life. I've had to pick him up from school several times now.

I just want to know what I'm missing in terms of resolving this.

Dear Mom,

All that is going on with your son, has to do with your energy and your fears. Your son is highly sensitive and therefore is able to view through his third eye, all your crystallized thought forms, which have to do with self-doubt and lack of courage to claim your space and truth.

Your son is there to draw your attention to this issue, because your inner world is so agitated. Your son has these elementals of yours invading his aura and becoming unsettled.

First of all, let us work with your energy field and clean your emotional body. You can get distance healing from me or my mother, or get someone you prefer to balance your chakras.

When you clean your energy bodies and work on altering your lifestyle, your son will become calmer and more settled.

I tell you, mom, start working on yourself, and then on your son's environment and space where he spends his time, and he will get better because he will not have to deal with less evolved forms of consciousness altering his vibration and frequency.

Love and light,
João Carlos

CHAPTER 16

Technology

Why does my 12-year old son only watch shows for 4-year olds and should we limit his time on his iPad?

My son wants to play on his iPad almost constantly. He wants to watch videos on the iPad or shows on TV that are not age appropriate. He likes shows that are for 4 or 5-year olds even though he is 12-years old.

I am concerned about the amount of time he wants to spend on his iPad and also the preschool programs he watches. I am not sure if it's better for my son to have very limited time on his iPad or allow him to play whenever he wants.

He doesn't include his family or anyone when he is on his iPad. Yet he constantly keeps asking for it when we limit it and doesn't really seem interested in anything else. What is best?

Dear Mom,

Your concern about the iPad seems right on the perspective of what catches the eye, but let me soothe you about what is really going on.

Your son loves his iPad because the light and colors on the screen turn down his brain receptors and he calms down, not being so prone to the sounds, light and smells around him that aggravate his sensory issues.

With his iPad he can focus and have a clear and restricted vision of the things on the screen, whereas when he does not look at the screen his vision field is overwhelming and petrifying, making him feel threatened and insecure.

He likes the children's programs, not only because of the sounds and colors, but also because children are very much connected to Source and have not become totally alienated from their true Self and formatted by society.

Your son feels closer to his true Self when watching these programs because adults have forgotten about their inner wisdom and power, and contrary to what they think, are very fragile and live by what is expected of them and not the voice within.

When you look at your son and want him to heal there is a part of yourself coming out of judgement, but when you embrace what seems to be the flaws, Love pervades every cell and balance is restored to the body, and what you call healing occurs.

Blessings,
João Carlos

Should we restrict use of electronic devices and light up toys for our son with autism?

My 14-year old son loves to play videos on my cell phone. He loves to watch the same video, over and over, of an air conditioner spinning around. I worry about the blue light devices as being bad for his brain. Should we stop him from playing on these devices?

He also loves to play with light up toys. That's all he does in his free time. Should we limit these too? Why does he love these so much?

Dear Mom,

Listen and see your son with your heart, and the answers you seek will be given to you. There is no need to stop the blue light and light up toys for him, because he sees in them focus and comfort from overwhelming surroundings.

The least resistance in regard to these that he feels, the less need he will have to seek refuge in them.

Blessings,
João Carlos

My 13-year old son is obsessed with video games. Is this because he is traumatized by the divorce and he is avoiding his feelings?

My son is a very kind and sensitive soul. He is not autistic, but his older brother is. I am worried about his mental health as it relates to the divorce. I have always felt like he is the peacekeeper and he takes on too much responsibility for those around him.

He also seems obsessed with video games and YouTube memes, he will watch them for hours by sneaking his computer into his room at night. Is this his way of avoiding feelings and issues? How can I help him here?

Dear Mom,

Your son is indeed a beautiful soul, but he also has a very different outlook on the divorce that you may not have perceived.

The way marriage and divorce is seen on Earth, is often one based on fear, so people try to find ways to get over that fear of lack of commitment, and therefore sign contracts of tying or untying (getting married or getting divorced).

Your son is not affected by the divorce and he may seem so because you are projecting it on him. It is your fear that you may have let him down, that gives you that idea.

Your son knows that the only energy that bonds is Love, and he knows that although apart, all is well. His parents have fulfilled their soul contract of having a family of three children, and now has come the time of walking different paths.

Tell your son that you are always happy with his outlook on life, even if it seems different to yours. As for the video games, look at what avoidance behaviors you have, and when you work on them, your son will look less evasive and will grow interest in other areas.

Blessings,
João Carlos

CHAPTER 17

Mental Health

Is my 9-year old son happy about the biomedical interventions, therapy and programs we are doing?

I have a son who is turning 9-years old in a few weeks. He is sweet, intelligent and hard-working. From day one, we have always acted based on the assumption that he heard and understood everything said in front of him. We do a lot of biomedical interventions and he is always resistant, but we have persisted for more than four years now.

I would love to know if he knows and feels that he is loved. Is he happy with his program, including all the therapies and interventions now, and the ones we have tried?

Does he like the people on his team? Who does he like the most? Does he feel that the biomedical interventions have helped him become a better version of himself?

Dear Mom,

First and foremost, how wonderful it is to know that there are people who continue to enhance the potential of individuals with autism.

Your son is a beautiful soul and can go a long way, provided he has the necessary conditions. Your son is a young boy with a sparkle in the eye and no doubt happy.

As for the people who work with him, not all are on the same page and that can sometimes be stressful. Pay attention to his reactions to certain people, for his eyes will let you know as they become dimmer, and his skin complexion tighter.

Therapies are good when balanced in terms of quantity and quality and so are biomedical interventions. Once again pay close attention to his body language and your intuition.

He is happy, but more does not always mean better.

Blessings,
João Carlos

How can we reduce my 11-year old daughter's anxiety?

My daughter was diagnosed with ASD when she was five. She is now eleven and receives ABA therapy at school in an "Intensive education" class as part of their special education program. She has speech, PT and OT to help her language and motor skills deficiencies.

Our biggest challenge is her anxiety which can brought on by one/more of several triggers- auditory processing difficulties (hyper-sensitive to sounds, esp. distress sounds of small children) and other sensory issues like tactile/texture/oral defensiveness.

In the school setting, her fear of "being put on the spot" when asked to do tasks that she's capable of leads to avoidant/non-compliant/defiant behavior.

Last year, almost all our parent-teacher meetings were about behavioral issues. I used to get the same feeling that João mentioned- her teacher seemed more intent on "fixing my daughter or fitting her into conformity" than on trying to understand her better. This year we have a new teacher who struck me as being a compassionate person. Thankfully my daughter is doing better with her- even starting to communicate and express herself. She seems to engage better with given tasks.

I've also noticed that among family members, my daughter seems more comfortable around certain people than others. So my question is, can she really perceive "intention" of the person with her? As for myself, I notice she is calmer and more engaging when I'm more calm and relaxed (not always easy to do given the stress of everyday life!).

How can I convince her of my own intention to help her progress towards independent living someday without coming across as too demanding? We certainly want her to be motivated towards improving her motor/language skills, but how can we expect this from her in a way that doesn't induce anxiety?

Dear Mom,

Thank you and blessings fall upon you, my dear mother. Your daughter is a beautiful and sensitive girl and most of what you ask, you know the answers.

Your daughter does pick up on the energy of people around her and on people's moods and you yourself have observed that she mirrors your mood, feels those who are less accepting and more judgmental.

At school acceptance and tolerance are crucial, so that she feels safe to risk new tasks.

Individuals with autism, many times, are very insecure because their body does not always follow the command of the brain, but also because people fail to understand this and put pressure - increasing anxiety.

What we should do is to soothe the person, let her grow in confidence by believing in her strengths and letting the person, in her own time, open to the task or project at hand.

When you push, you encounter resistance and when you surrender, you give space to surprise.

Blessings,
João Carlos

What did I do wrong to cause my 9-year old son to severely regress this past year?

My son has ASD and now he is 9-years old. He has regressed badly in these past 8 months. He is now experiencing insomnia, severe anxiety, phobia, scared of sunlight and terrible OCD's.

What did I do wrong in the course of healing my son?

Why is he having the above issues, when he has been showing steady progress since he was 4-years old?

Is it the school? My broken marriage? Or the current house we are staying in? (We are now staying with my parents in a village) Or is it the supplements?

Dear Mom,

First of all, blessings and thank you for writing. The insight I get in regard to you and your son, is that a lot of challenges have crossed your path. However, all is really leading you in the right direction, despite not quite looking as so.

Your son is a very sensitive being and as such, picks up on fearful thoughts and limiting beliefs. He does have sensory issues and you have to look into his current treatment, but there are profound changes that you as a mother have to undergo, for he is reflecting the energy and vibration of all that surrounds him.

There is the need for you to forgive yourself, for you did no wrong in his healing path. You did what you thought best, according to what you knew or believed in. But now that the old has all collapsed, there needs to be the incoming of transparent energy.

There is the need for you to look at your son with a new perspective, and that can only be done by working on yourself, and recognizing all that you have and have forgotten, to love. Look inside. Meditation will help and so will energy healing.

Tell yourself each day, looking into the mirror, that you love yourself. Tell your son, in the eyes, that he does not need to inflict pain upon himself, for he is Love and much loved.

Blessings,
João Carlos

How does a mother let go of grief and sorrow?

I have been struggling with feeling the grief and sorrow associated with my son's autism diagnosis. I have blamed myself and also felt guilty for not preventing it.

It feels so overwhelming and I'm not sure how to let go of it.

Dear Mom,

In the first place I would like to tell you that all is well. Look beyond the grief and you will be able to find peace in your heart.

One of the suggestions that I have for you is to forgive yourself. How can you do this every day?

Go for a walk in a park and as you do so envision yourself connecting to trees and their energy. If you are open to the idea embrace one with your chest against it and set your intention to release the pain and to receive the healing energy of the tree. As you do, open your heart chakra and repeat:

"I allow myself to set free my sorrow and receive Love and healing energy. I am Love and all that comes to me is Love. And so it is."

When you are at home envision yourself surrounded by violet light and repeat:

"All that comes into my energy field is Love and only Love."

Be blessed and feel blessed,
João Carlos

CHAPTER 18

Wellness

Why is my 9-year old son so resistant to my suggestions for healthy food choices?

My son had an interesting entrance into this world. I was turning 40-years old after my second son was born, and I had a tubal ligation so I couldn't get pregnant at my advanced age. Well along he came anyway, when I was 43-years old. His personality matches his willfulness to be a part of our family.

How can I support his emotional wellbeing? He is so quick to anger when anyone tells him what to do. He wants to make all of his own decisions. I know that's good on many levels, but not for everything.

He fights me on nutrition and wants to eat all junk food. Naturally I don't stock junk food, but he'll eat it any chance he gets, at school or outside the home. It's almost as if whatever I say, he will only do the opposite. He has always been an autonomous boy - no one can tell him what to do! Any thoughts on supporting him?

Dear Mom,

Here are my insights. Your son is here to show you that despite the odds, what seems impossible becomes possible.

There is an energy of rejection or non-acceptance, which you have to work on.

Of course, we have to be mindful of what we eat, but most important is the energy you put into the food when you eat. If you eat out of the energy of having to, or of guilt, you are imbuing your body with that energy.

Whatever you resist persists. If you start looking at food with a more neutral mindset, you will open space for eating habits which are healthier, and get your son to willingly favor other options. Opposing his choice leads him to feel non-respected in his choices, and clinging onto them longer.

Blessings,
João Carlos

What is triggering the seizures in my 13-year old son?

My son is 13-years old and non-verbal. He had encephalitis as an infant, and has seizures since he was one year old. He has five to fifteen seizures a month.

About three years ago we removed all medications. He had some improvement with dietary interventions but inconsistently. The seizures affect him greatly. He loses complete control of his body and is exhausted for days to weeks after.

I would appreciate if you can connect with him and give me some insight on how he feels and what triggers his seizures.

Is it only food? Is he very sensitive to people's emotions?

Dear Mom,

Blessings to you and your beloved son. Let me start by telling you, that despite all the pain an individual may feel, whether physical or not, it is all part of a higher plan and things are always where they are supposed to be, with your Inner Being always guiding you to become a more awakened human.

Your son, as a soul, made soul contracts with other souls, including the members of his family, and all is to lead you to awakening, for there is no more delaying on this planet. As such you either increase frequency and vibration, or remain dormant in the third dimension.

Your son is a sensitive soul with a very high frequency that has difficulty adjusting to the third-dimension energy, and therefore he has seizures. He wants to ground, but the energy around him makes it difficult.

What's needed is a bigger match between his energy and that of his parents, to reduce seizures and to relieve the pain he inflicts on himself for not having yet managed to draw his parents towards spiritual awakening.

Find your inner peace and let it surface.

Blessings,
João Carlos

What does my 10-year old daughter want me to know about her wellbeing and integration?

I would love to hear your perspective about my 10-year old daughter with autism. She is entering puberty, and I am supporting her on many levels, but it would be very useful to hear from you.

What does my daughter's soul want me to know, that would be useful for her communication, health, development of her full potential, living with purpose and reaching her dreams and goals?

Dear Mom,

As you know, and can easily tune in, your daughter is a highly evolved soul who decided to volunteer to come to this plane to evolve. Her soul and wellbeing and integration, depend on a wide variety of factors, among them acceptance and awakening of those around her.

You are on your spiritual path, but a whole lot more is needed. When I speak of acceptance, I do not mean just letting things be, but rather your daughter being looked at by all those around her, as a soul with a different manifestation on Earth, and not one who is looked upon with pity.

When all souls are looked on as valuable souls with something to share, to others it is a good way to help integration. Integration does not occur with non-acceptance, especially with autistic individuals who feel too much pain from the collective on this plane.

As for the school setting that would favor your daughter, pick one with the energy of acceptance, and that does not run on the energy of formatting.

Unlike what is believed, autistic individuals have a lot of knowledge to share, and schools have to have that space for them to flourish. Your daughter needs such a setting.

Love and light,
João Carlos

Why am I here?

I am a 46-year old mother with two children, my daughter has autism. I would like to know why I am here?

I would like to communicate telepathically with my children and I have been trying for a long time. Sometimes I am able to connect with other autistic kids, but not reliably.

I am having difficulty staying positive. I am feeling stuck in common consciousness (people soup). At times, I am angry and judgmental, when I want to be light filled.

What is meant when my autistic daughter says "yellow mom" (while seeing something energetically on my cheek area).

I also have health concerns. I have severe bone loss in my bottom jaw and I fear there is a danger of me losing my teeth. I am wondering if this is indicative of the bone status in the rest of my body. I have sore feet that make it difficult to walk at times.

Dear Mom,

The answer to your first question is that we are consciousness deriving from a greater source or supreme consciousness. As souls we want to evolve, and in order for that to occur, we reincarnate to grow through experiences and learning. We all come with a mission and soul purpose, and your children are souls which have come to assist in your growth.

We can all communicate telepathically, but because some people have forgotten how, the process has to be relearned, like with yourself. Practice sitting still and creating a void in your mind, so that seeing things and listening can move to a different level.

As for being judgmental and angry, try to lighten your diet and avoid toxic people and contexts.

Your daughter refers to "yellow mom" because there is a lot of rage and loss of personal power within you.

Your bone issues have got to do with fear of expression and loss of structure.

Love and light,
João Carlos

How can I reconnect to my intuitive self?

I feel like I am having trouble connecting to my intuition. I would like to listen to my inner guidance but I feel at a loss as to how to go about it.

Do you have any insights?

Dear Mom,

The first thing one of the Angels is whispering is, that you have been hiding from yourself from some time.

As a young child, you were very much connected and intuitive, yet that part of you was not very deeply accepted and you shut down.

Come to terms that we are all taken care of, and all we have to do is trust the process, and ask for help when we need it. I suggest that you begin by looking within, and listening to the messages that come through.

Close your eyes every morning or end of day, and ask out loud to the Angels or Beings of Light what you want to know. Then repeat three times:

"I am open to receiving answers from the Light."

Sit in silence for a few minutes with an open mind and heart. The thoughts, words or images that occur, write them down when you open your eyes. You will understand the meaning sometime after.

Trust the process and trust yourself.

You are very much loved and we welcome you.

Blessings my dear one,
João Carlos

Afterword

If you take one thing away from this book, I hope it is this. All is well. That doesn't mean that life is easy, or that having a child with autism is not challenging. But the truth of what is actually going on is simple and the answers point to one path.

Work on yourself, and your child will respond.

João is a compassionate, intuitive young man, trapped inside a body that often fails him. He lives from the energy of Love, a frequency and vibration that is mismatched to the density of this planet, where fear still rules. And so it is with many of our children who present with autism. It is the reason they struggle in our world and we cannot seem to connect with them.

The solution to helping them becomes crystal clear when we consider the mismatch, raise the vibration of yourself and their environment, and they can more readily assimilate here on Earth.

You have nothing to lose, and everything to gain, if you will just take a leap of faith in the power of Love.

Made in the USA
San Bernardino, CA
22 June 2020